Orient Express

Orient Express
Silvena Rowe

Photographs by Jonathan Lovekin

HUTCHINSON

LONDON

Published by Hutchinson 2011

10 9 8 7 6 5 4 3 2 1

Copyright © Silvena Rowe 2011

Photographs © Jonathan Lovekin

First published in Great Britain in 2011 by Hutchinson
Random House, 20 Vauxhall Bridge Road, London SW1V 2SA

www.rbooks.co.uk

Addresses for companies within The Random House Group Limited can be found at:
www.randomhouse.co.uk/offices.htm

The Random House Group Limited Reg. No. 954009

A CIP catalogue record for this book
is available from the British Library

ISBN 9780091930950

Commissioning Editor: Emma Rose
Designer: Richard Marston
Cover designer: Emma Grey
Production: Phil Brown
Stylist: Susie Theodorou
Copy-editor: Annie Lee

The Random House Group Limited supports The Forest Stewardship Council (FSC),
the leading international forest certification organisation. All our titles that are printed
on Greenpeace approved FSC certified paper carry the FSC logo. Our paper procurement
policy can be found at www.rbooks.co.uk/environment

Printed and bound by Firmengruppe APPL, aprinta druck, Wemding, Germany

To Mama

Contents

Introduction   vii

Chef's Note   ix

Emerald Spice & Gold Dust

Za'atar and Saffron

I

Fire & Noble Velvet

Chilli and Cumin

37

Purple Citrus & Summer Breeze

Sumac and Fresh Herbs

78

Sweet Eucalyptus & Liquid Gold

Cardamom and Honey

127

Exotic Perfume & Delicate Fragrances

Cinnamon and Flowers

151

Essential Accompaniments and Spice Blends   169

The Eastern Mediterranean Store-cupboard   182

Index   184

Acknowledgements   192

How fair is thy love, my sister, my spouse! how much better is thy love than wine!
and the smell of thine ointments than all spices!

Thy lips, O my spouse, drop as the honeycomb: honey and milk are under thy tongue;
and the smell of thy garments is like the smell of Lebanon.

A garden inclosed is my sister, my spouse; a spring shut up, a fountain sealed.

Thy plants are an orchard of pomegranates, with pleasant fruits; camphire,
with spikenard,

Spikenard and saffron; calamus and cinnamon, with all trees of frankincense;
myrrh and aloes, with all the chief spices.

The Song of Solomon 4:10–14

Chef's Note

At the end of this book I've included an essential accompaniments and spice blends section. It includes my own simple recipes for Eastern Mediterranean essentials such as za'atar and baharat, as well as easy instructions for making pomegranate molasses, another Eastern Mediterranean cooking staple. There's also a section on the Eastern Mediterranean store-cupboard, which suggests some staples needed for the recipes in this book and explains some of the more unusual ingredients.

All herbs listed in the ingredients are dried and ground, unless otherwise stated. When I refer to a large or small bunch of fresh herbs this is a rough guide to what you'll be able to find in your greengrocer's – when using fresh herbs, most of the time you can use as much as you wish to bring the flavour out. When a smaller quantity is required for a more subtle flavour I've indicated that you use a 50g pack instead, which I find is the standard size available in supermarkets.

When it comes to olive oil, I always use the best-quality extra virgin oil I can find, as this will always have the most satisfying flavour. But it's fine to use whatever olive oil you have to hand. I also often recommend cooking with clarified butter (ghee), which is bought in liquid form and doesn't burn as easily or turn brown.

I season a lot of my dishes with freshly ground sea salt and black pepper. Always use as little or as much as suits your tastes.

Finally, cooking times are shown in degrees centigrade (for fan-assisted ovens) and gas mark. For non-fan-assisted ovens add 20 degrees to the temperature indicated.

Emerald Spice & Gold Dust

ZA'ATAR AND SAFFRON

Za'atar (pronounced za-ah-ta) is a blend of herbs and spices used in cooking through-out the Eastern Mediterranean region. Many chefs have their own secret recipes and, no matter how hard you try (and believe me, I've tried everything), they will never divulge it to you.

In general it is made up of ground sumac, toasted sesame seeds and dried green herbs, usually thyme and oregano, which give it that rich emerald colour. The flavour is hard to describe, because with so many 'secret' ingredients, it can be tangy, zesty or nutty.

Making your own za'atar at home is simple. I have my own favourite blend named after my new restaurant, Quince, (see page 180), but if you don't have time, it is available to buy ready blended. Za'atar can be used to flavour lamb or chicken, it can be sprinkled on roasted vegetables and pastries and it can even be mixed with a little olive oil and drizzled on bread.

Saffron comes from the saffron crocus flower and is made by drying the tiny threads of the flower's stigmas. It is, quite literally, like gold dust, as it's the most expensive spice (by weight) in the world, more expensive than gold. Fortunately, when cooking with saffron, less is more. Crushed and soaked in warm water or white wine for at least five minutes, only a few threads will make a huge difference. And the deep golden yellow colour is something to behold when creating dishes.

The unique floral yet slightly bitter taste of saffron works particularly well in home-made mayonnaise and aioli, or when combined with cumin and mellow paprika. But never be tempted to use too much, as it can overpower a dish and leave it with a slightly medicinal taste.

Spiced Quail and Foie Gras Filo Parcels

These wonderful cute and tasty pies are not dissimilar to those known as bisteeya in North Africa. Fast food at its best, you can also make these with chicken or pigeon. It's one of my signature dishes for my Quince chef's table.

4 quails, approx. 200g each

3 tablespoons olive oil

2 shallots, sliced

2 garlic cloves, crushed

2cm fresh ginger, peeled and finely chopped

6 saffron threads

½ teaspoon ground cumin

½ teaspoon chilli flakes

40ml cognac or brandy

250ml chicken stock

small bunch of fresh thyme with flowers, chopped

10 sheets of filo pastry (standard supermarket-bought size)

100g fresh foie gras, cubed

100g pistachios, toasted and finely chopped

20g melted butter

3 tablespoons icing sugar

Preheat the oven to 180°C fan/gas mark 6.

Wash the quails and pat them dry with a clean cloth. Separate the legs from the breasts, and season the pieces. In a large heavy pan, sauté all the quail pieces in the olive oil on a high heat for 2–3 minutes, browning on all sides. Add the shallots, garlic, ginger, saffron, cumin and chilli flakes. Reduce the heat and add the cognac, taking care not to set it alight. Finally, stir in the stock. Cover and cook on low to medium heat for 45 minutes, until the quail is tender. Remove from heat and allow to cool.

Put aside the cooking juices. Remove the meat from the quail pieces and discard the bones and skin. Shred the meat and place in a bowl. Return the cooking liquid to a medium heat and simmer for another 10–15 minutes, until the liquid has reduced to a quarter. Now stir in the fresh thyme and shredded meat, season and cook for a final 2–3 minutes.

Lay out a sheet of filo pastry (you need sheets that are approx. 20 × 10cm in size). Lay a second sheet on top of the first. Cut the two layers in half so you're left with two double-thick squares. Repeat with the remaining 8 filo sheets until you have 10 squares in total. Brush with a little melted butter and in the centre of each square place a generous spoonful of the quail mixture, top with a cube of the foie gras and finally sprinkle with some chopped pistachio. Fold in the corners of each square to make 10 small parcels.

Arrange the parcels on a baking sheet, seam side down. Brush the tops with the melted butter and bake for 10–12 minutes, until golden. Remove and dust with the icing sugar.

Makes 10

Baby Carrot, Orange and Za'atar Hummus

450g baby carrots, peeled
1 large onion, sliced
3 garlic cloves, crushed
4 tablespoons olive oil
3 tablespoons orange juice
zest of 1 orange
1 tablespoon za'atar
3 teaspoons ground cumin
1 tablespoon tahini

TO SERVE
1 teaspoon tahini
2 tablespoons tinned chickpeas, drained

Preheat the oven to 200°C fan/gas mark 7.

Spread out the carrots, onions and garlic in an ovenproof dish, drizzle with olive oil and add a cup of water. Cover the dish with foil and roast the vegetables for 25–30 minutes, until cooked. Remove the vegetables from the oven and allow to cool.

Place the cooked vegetables in a food processor. Add the orange juice, orange zest, za'atar, cumin and tahini. Process until smooth and season to taste.

Spoon into a serving bowl, drizzle with the extra tahini and sprinkle the chickpeas on top.

For 6 to share

Börek Rolls with Crab, Saffron and Fennel

I love crab and I love börek, so this is my ideal snack! Börek, a Turkish stuffed pastry, is traditionally prepared with meat, offal or vegetables, but using fresh white crabmeat, perfumed with a touch of saffron, makes this a thoroughly modern sultan of böreks.

300g fresh white crabmeat, cooked

2–3 fresh tarragon sprigs, finely chopped

1 large fennel bulb, finely sliced

6 spring onions, finely sliced

2 tablespoons olive oil

6 saffron threads, crushed

½ teaspoon ground sumac

½ teaspoon brown sugar

zest of 1 lemon

juice of ½ lemon

12 sheets of filo pastry + extra in case they break

2 tablespoons melted butter

½ teaspoon ground sumac (extra, for garnish)

Preheat the oven to 180°C fan/gas mark 6.

Place the cooked crabmeat in a bowl, add the tarragon, cover and refrigerate until needed.

In a pan, sauté the sliced fennel and spring onions in the olive oil on a low to medium heat for 15 minutes. Add the saffron, sumac and sugar. Season and cook for a further 3–4 minutes, until the fennel is caramelised and still moist. Stir in the lemon zest and juice and remove from the heat. Allow to cool, then add the crabmeat and tarragon, combine well and season again if required.

Use one sheet of filo pastry for each börek cigar. Fold into thirds, so that you have a thin rectangle about 10cm wide. Brush with a little melted butter and spoon some of the filling on to one end. Roll once to seal in the filling. Fold in the sides and continue to roll (as if making a spring roll). Repeat with the remaining pastry sheets and filling. Arrange the rolls on a baking sheet, seam side down. Brush the tops with the remaining butter and sprinkle with sumac. Bake in the oven for 10–20 minutes, until golden brown.

Makes 12

Za'atar Spiced Rabbit Gözleme

Gözleme are a favourite in Turkey, a sort of pastry sandwich, sold everywhere from street corners to sophisticated restaurants and usually prepared with local cheese or lamb. For something more distinctive I love to make them with rabbit.

2 tablespoons olive oil

1 large onion, sliced

3 garlic cloves, crushed

1 rabbit, jointed into small pieces

1 teaspoon ground cumin

1 teaspoon ground paprika

½ teaspoon ground allspice

¼ teaspoon ground cardamom

1 teaspoon za'atar, plus extra for garnish

100ml dry white wine

200ml chicken stock

small bunch of fresh oregano, finely chopped

3 tablespoons melted butter

3 tablespoons olive oil (extra)

3 large circular sheets of yufka or filo pastry

1–2 tablespoons melted clarified butter or ghee

Preheat the oven to 180°C fan/gas mark 6.

Heat the olive oil in a large ovenproof casserole dish. Add the onion, garlic and rabbit pieces and cook for about 5 minutes, until the meat is browned on all sides. Stir in the cumin, paprika, allspice, cardamom, za'atar, white wine and chicken stock. Simmer for 5 minutes, then cover and cook in the oven for 45 minutes.

Remove the rabbit from the casserole dish and allow to cool completely before shredding the meat and discarding the skin and bones. Meanwhile, return the casserole dish, with its cooking juices, to the hob, bring to the boil and reduce until a third of the liquid has evaporated. Then stir in the shredded meat and fresh oregano. Remove from the heat.

Combine the melted butter and olive oil in a small bowl. Lay 3 circular sheets of yufka pastry on top of each other and cut in half. Lay the halves on top of each other and cut into 4 equal wedges, so that you end up with 24 in total. Now cut off the rounded edges at the top of each wedge so that you have 24 triangles.

Brush some oil and butter on to one of the pastry triangles, spoon on some of the rabbit mixture and top with another pastry triangle. Seal down the edges, brush with some more oil and butter, then sprinkle with the extra za'atar (see overleaf). Repeat until you have 12 filled pastries.

To cook, brush a frying pan with the clarified butter and when medium hot, sauté the gözleme for about 1 minute on each side, until golden and crispy.

Makes 12

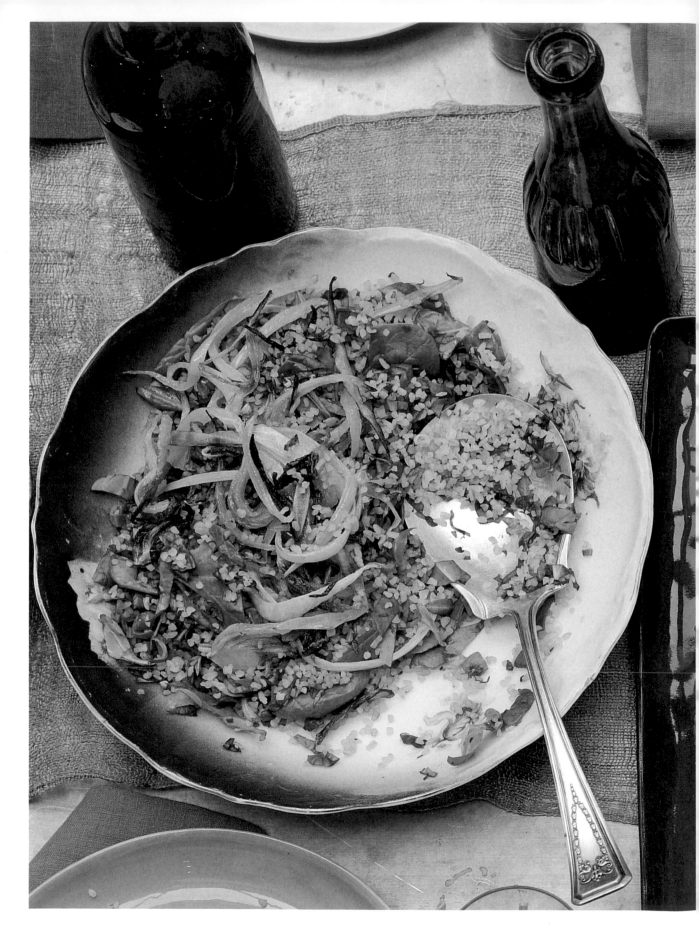

Swiss Chard Bulgur Pilaf with Caramelised Fennel and Za'atar

Most people wouldn't think of a pilaf as a snack, but it was in my house. I didn't eat a sandwich until I was about sixteen! A rice pilaf with spinach was always a favourite, but there were variations: purslane, Swiss chard, sometimes even dandelion leaves. Pilafs are always best served with a dollop of chilled yoghurt.

FOR THE CARAMELISED FENNEL

- 1 medium fennel bulb, finely sliced
- 1 onion, finely sliced
- 3 tablespoons olive oil
- 10g butter
- zest and juice of 1 small lemon

FOR THE PILAF

- 4 spring onions, chopped
- 2 tablespoons olive oil
- 350g coarse bulgur
- 500ml chicken or vegetable stock
- 400g Swiss chard leaves, chopped

TO MAKE THE CARAMELISED FENNEL

In a pan, sauté the fennel and onion in the olive oil on a low to medium heat for 10–15 minutes, stirring from time to time, until they are soft and caramelised. Remove from the heat and add the butter, lemon zest and juice. Stir until the butter has melted, then put to one side.

TO MAKE THE PILAF

In a large heavy pan, sauté the spring onions in the olive oil on a medium heat for 3–4 minutes. Stir in the bulgur until the grains are well coated. Now pour in the stock, cover and cook on a low to medium heat for 15–20 minutes, until the bulgur is soft. A few minutes before the bulgur is cooked, add the Swiss chard and season to taste.

Serve the pilaf topped with the caramelised fennel.

For 8 to share

Saffron Yoghurt Chicken
with Cumin Salt Aioli

8 chicken thighs, skin and
bones removed

FOR THE MARINADE

400ml plain yoghurt

8 saffron threads

2 garlic cloves, crushed

1 teaspoon ground cumin

3cm fresh ginger, peeled and
finely grated

FOR THE AIOLI

½ teaspoon cumin seeds

¼ teaspoon sea salt

2 egg yolks

1 garlic clove, crushed

zest of 1 lemon

150ml light olive oil

1 DAY IN ADVANCE

Combine the marinade ingredients in a bowl. Add the chicken and coat well.
Cover and refrigerate for a minimum of 4 hours, or preferably overnight.

TO COOK THE CHICKEN

Preheat a non-stick griddle pan or grill to high and cook the chicken for
10–12 minutes on each side, until cooked right through.

TO MAKE THE AIOLI

Place the cumin seeds and sea salt in a spice grinder (or use a mortar and
pestle) and grind until almost powdered. Whisk the egg yolks (make sure you
use top-quality fresh free-range eggs) in a bowl and add the garlic and lemon
zest, whisking all the time. Drizzle in the olive oil until you have achieved the
consistency of double cream (you may find that you don't use all the oil).
Finally, stir in the cumin salt.

Serve the chicken hot, with the cumin salt aioli.

For 8 to share

Kadaifi-Wrapped Aubergine with Za'atar Rouille

Kadaifi pastry is like shredded filo pastry. It looks like a lot of loose strands and is generally used for wrapping sweet or savoury fillings. Work fast because the pastry dries quickly – cover it with a damp cloth when you're not working it. Rouille is a Mediterranean sauce usually made with breadcrumbs. My twist on this classic is to use sweet potato.

FOR THE ROUILLE

- 1 large sweet potato, peeled and cubed
- 3 garlic cloves, chopped
- 1 green chilli, de-seeded and roughly chopped
- 2cm fresh ginger, peeled and roughly chopped
- 1 tablespoon za'atar
- juice of ½ lemon
- 100ml olive oil

FOR THE AUBERGINE

- 2 medium aubergines
- 200g kadaifi pastry
- vegetable oil, for deep-frying

TO MAKE THE ROUILLE

Cook the sweet potato in a pan of boiling water for about 20 minutes, until soft. Drain and allow to cool. Using a food processor, blend the garlic, chilli and ginger to a paste. Add the sweet potato, za'atar and lemon juice, and season to taste. With the food processor running, slowly drizzle in the olive oil until you achieve a creamy, silky-smooth purée.

TO PREPARE THE AUBERGINES

Slice the aubergines in half lengthways, then into 1cm thick pieces widthways. Lay some strands of kadaifi pastry on your work surface. Place a piece of aubergine at one end of the pastry and roll it up in the pastry. Repeat with the rest of the aubergine pieces.

TO COOK THE AUBERGINES

Heat the vegetable oil in a deep-fat fryer to 180°C. Using heatproof tongs, place 2 wrapped aubergine pieces in the hot oil and cook for 2 minutes, until golden and crispy. Remove and place on kitchen paper to drain. Repeat until you have cooked all the aubergine pieces.

Serve hot, with the za'atar rouille.

For 8 to share

Langoustine Salad with Preserved Lemon and Za'atar Butter

FOR THE BUTTER

1 onion, sliced

2 garlic cloves, crushed

1 teaspoon olive oil

1 tablespoon za'atar

1 preserved lemon, skin only, finely chopped

small bunch of fresh thyme, finely chopped

150g butter, softened

FOR THE LANGOUSTINES

16 large langoustines, shells removed

2 tablespoons olive oil

generous pinch of sea salt

½ tablespoon sumac

FOR THE SALAD

small bunch of fresh chives

12 red radishes, sliced paper-thin

1 red onion, peeled and sliced paper-thin

10 large green olives, stoned and roughly chopped

TO MAKE THE BUTTER

In a pan, sauté the onion and garlic in the olive oil on a low heat for 5 minutes, until soft and mushy but not brown. Stir in the za'atar, preserved lemon and thyme. Remove from the heat and allow to cool. Place the onion and garlic mix in a bowl and work in the softened butter. Shape into a sausage, wrap in clingfilm and refrigerate until needed.

TO COOK THE LANGOUSTINES

In a pan, sauté the langoustines in 2 tablespoons of olive oil on a medium heat for 2–3 minutes. Season with the sea salt and sumac.

TO MAKE THE SALAD

Chop the chives into 2cm slices, keeping the flowers intact. Combine the salad ingredients in a bowl. Spoon some on to each plate and top with a couple of langoustines. Melt a third of the preserved lemon and za'atar butter in a small pan and pour over the top of the langoustines. Serve immediately.

For 8 to share

Watermelon and Cherry Tomato Salad with Feta, Almond and Za'atar Crumble

There is nothing that reminds me more of home than watermelons, great mountains of them piled up in the market. And there is nothing better than a heavily chilled watermelon slice on a hot summer afternoon. With this in mind I created this salad. It's very simple and absolutely delicious. Make sure you use perfectly ripe watermelon and tomatoes.

FOR THE SALAD

½ medium watermelon, peeled and cut into chunky cubes

200g cherry tomatoes, halved

small bunch of fresh mint, leaves only

FOR THE CRUMBLE

200g feta cheese, crumbled

100g almonds, lightly toasted and crushed

1 teaspoon za'atar

TO SERVE

fresh bread

white nasturtiums or if unavailable use herb flowers

Combine the salad ingredients in a large serving bowl. Mix together the crumble ingredients and sprinkle on top of the salad. Sprinkle with white nasturtium flowers. Serve with fresh bread.

For 8 to share

Duck and Black Sesame Za'atar Kleftiko

1 large duck

1 tablespoon olive oil

½ teaspoon ground cinnamon

2 bay leaves

4 large potatoes, peeled and cubed

2 lemons, cut in wedges

FOR THE ZA'ATAR

1 tablespoon black sesame seeds

½ tablespoon sumac

½ tablespoon cumin seeds

1 small bunch lemon thyme, leaves only

salt and pepper

TO SERVE

200g fresh wild rocket leaves

Preheat the oven to 140°C fan/gas mark 3.

For the za'atar, toast the sesame seeds lightly with the cumin seeds. Cool and grind in blender or pestle. Add sumac and lemon thyme leaves. Blend and season to taste.

Line a large oven tray with enough foil to make a sort of tent over the duck. Place the duck whole on the foil, season and drizzle with the olive oil. Sprinkle on the za'atar and cinnamon, scatter over the bay leaves, and arrange the potatoes – all under the duck if possible, that way they cook best! – and lemon wedges around the base. Pull the foil over the duck, making sure it is sealed on all sides. Roast in the oven for 3½ hours.

When ready, take the tray out of the oven and carefully unfold the foil. Cook for 30 more minutes at 180°C. Cool, shred the meat, discarding bones and skin.

Serve the shredded duck with the warm potatoes and wild rocket leaves.

For 6 to share

Za'atar-Crumbed Prawn and Sweet Potato Cakes

500g sweet potatoes, peeled and cubed

1 onion, finely chopped

½ teaspoon ground cumin

1 green chilli, de-seeded and chopped

2 garlic cloves, crushed

150g raw king prawns, shelled and cut into small chunks

4 tablespoons olive oil

5 tablespoons breadcrumbs

small bunch of fresh coriander, finely chopped

flour for dusting

4 tablespoons za'atar

5 tablespoons breadcrumbs (extra)

5–6 tablespoons olive oil (extra)

TO SERVE

tahini, sumac and lemon sauce (see p. 175 for the recipe)

Cook the sweet potatoes in boiling water for about 20 minutes, until soft. Drain and roughly mash, then season. In a pan, sauté the onion, cumin, chilli, garlic and prawns in 4 tablespoons of olive oil on a high heat, for 2–3 minutes. Remove from the heat and allow to cool for a few minutes in a mixing bowl. Add the sweet potato mash and fold in 5 tablespoons of breadcrumbs and the coriander. Cover and refrigerate for 30 minutes.

The mixture will be quite sticky, so when you're ready, flour your hands and shape into 20 little balls, then pat them down into oval-shaped cakes. Combine the za'atar and the second 5 tablespoons of breadcrumbs in a shallow dish. Coat the cakes in the breadcrumb mix, then place on a separate plate ready to fry.

Heat the extra olive oil in a large pan and fry the cakes, a few at a time, on a high heat. Place on kitchen paper to drain.

Serve hot with Tahini, Sumac and Lemon Sauce.

Makes 20

Za'atar Crispy Fried Calamari
with a Spicy Walnut Cream

FOR THE CREAM

2 shallots, finely sliced

1 tablespoon olive oil

100g fresh shelled walnuts

1 tablespoon fresh
breadcrumbs

1 tablespoon chilli paste

1 teaspoon tomato purée

1 tablespoon pomegranate
molasses (see p.175 for the
recipe)

2 tablespoons olive oil (extra)

½ teaspoon hot paprika

FOR THE CALAMARI

2 large egg whites

1 medium-sized fresh squid,
approx. 800g

6 tablespoons flour

4 tablespoons za'atar

vegetable oil, for deep-frying

TO MAKE THE CREAM

In a small pan, sauté the shallots in 1 tablespoon of olive oil for 2–3 minutes on a medium heat, until golden. Allow to cool slightly. In a food processor, blend the walnuts, breadcrumbs, chilli paste, tomato purée and molasses, until you have a smooth consistency. Add the cooked shallots and while still blending, drizzle in a little of the extra olive oil to achieve a thick creamy consistency. Finally, add the paprika, season to taste and chill until needed.

TO PREPARE THE CALAMARI

Lightly beat the egg whites in a bowl. Slice the squid into 1cm thick rings and drop into the egg white, making sure the rings are well coated. In a separate bowl, combine the flour and za'atar, then drop in the egg-coated squid rings, making sure they are now well coated with the za'atar mix.

TO COOK THE CALAMARI

Heat the vegetable oil in a deep-fat fryer to 180°C. Carefully drop the squid rings, a few at a time, into the hot oil and cook for 1 minute, until golden brown. Remove with a slotted wooden spoon and place on kitchen paper to drain. It's best to avoid cooking too many rings at once, as it reduces the temperature of the oil and the calamari won't crisp up as well.

Serve hot, with the spicy walnut cream.

For 8 to share

Spiced Lamb Filo Cigars with Za'atar and Pistachio Cream

FOR THE LAMB

1 teaspoon olive oil

350g lamb neck fillet, cubed

3cm fresh ginger, peeled and finely chopped

2 celery sticks, chopped

1 carrot, finely chopped

2 garlic cloves, crushed

2 green chillies, de-seeded and finely chopped

100ml lamb stock

1 teaspoon ras-el-hanout (see p.183)

salt and pepper

FOR THE CREAM

100ml double cream

1 teaspoon za'atar

50g pack of fresh oregano, leaves only, finely chopped

25g pistachios, finely ground

25g pistachios, roughly chopped

FOR THE CIGARS

12–14 sheets of filo pastry

2 tablespoons melted clarified butter or ghee

TO COOK THE LAMB

Preheat the oven to 180°C fan/gas mark 6.

Heat the olive oil in an ovenproof casserole dish on the hob. Add the lamb whole and cook for 10 minutes, turning until brown on all sides. Add the ginger, celery, carrot, garlic and chillies, and continue to sauté for 3–4 minutes before stirring in the stock. Cover and cook in the oven for about 45 minutes, until the lamb is tender and cooked. Remove from the oven and allow to cool.

Once cool enough to handle, shred the lamb into a bowl. Remove the vegetables from the casserole dish using a slotted spoon and add these to the lamb, mashing gently to combine with the meat. Sprinkle with ras-el-hanout, and season to taste.

TO MAKE THE CREAM

Whip the cream and add the za'atar, oregano and both the ground and chopped pistachios. Combine well and season to taste.

TO MAKE THE FILO CIGARS

Cut the filo sheets roughly into 10 × 10cm squares. Spoon some of the lamb filling along one side, not too near the edge. Roll once to seal in the filling. Fold in the sides, then continue to roll into a cigar shape. Use a little butter to seal the top edge down. Repeat with the remaining pastry sheets and filling. Arrange the cigars on a baking tray, seam side down. Brush with the remaining butter and bake in the oven for 10–20 minutes, until golden brown.

Serve hot with the whipped za'atar and pistachio cream.

For 8 to share

Turkey and Pine Nut Kebabs
with Saffron Mayonnaise

FOR THE MAYONNAISE

2 egg yolks

200ml light olive oil

1 tablespoon mild mustard paste

juice of 1 small lemon

4 saffron threads, soaked in 1 tablespoon of water

FOR THE KEBABS

400g turkey, minced

3 garlic cloves, crushed

¼ teaspoon ground cardamom

1 teaspoon ground cumin

3cm fresh ginger, peeled and grated

½ tablespoon chilli paste

small bunch of fresh coriander, finely chopped

4 tablespoons pine nuts

TO MAKE THE MAYONNAISE

Whisk the egg yolks in a bowl, continuing to whisk as you gradually drizzle in the olive oil until you have a thick, smooth and creamy mixture. Add the mustard, lemon juice and saffron, combine and season to taste.

TO MAKE THE KEBABS

Combine the turkey in a bowl with the garlic, cardamom, cumin, ginger, chilli paste and coriander, and season to taste. Shape into 16 small oval patties, about 5–6cm wide. Firmly roll them in the chopped pine nuts and cook under a high grill for 4–5 minutes on each side or longer, until cooked.

Serve hot, with the saffron mayonnaise.

For 8 to share

Orange and Za'atar Marinated Haloumi with Tomato and Za'atar Dressing

2 garlic cloves, crushed

2 tablespoons olive oil

1 tablespoon za'atar

zest and juice of 1 orange

300g haloumi cheese, cut into slices

FOR THE DRESSING

2 large ripe tomatoes, skinned and very finely chopped

3 tablespoons olive oil

1 shallot, grated

1 teaspoon runny honey

1 garlic clove, crushed

3 tablespoons white wine vinegar

1 tablespoon za'atar

TO SERVE

a few purple basil cress leaves

2 HOURS IN ADVANCE

Combine the garlic, olive oil, za'atar and orange juice and zest. Place the haloumi in a bowl and cover with the mixture, making sure that the cheese is completely coated. Marinate in the fridge for at least 2 hours or overnight.

TO COOK THE HALOUMI

Using a heavy non-stick pan, fry the haloumi cubes on a medium heat for 3 minutes on each side, until golden all over.

TO MAKE THE DRESSING

Simply combine all the ingredients in a bowl and season to taste. Drizzle over the hot haloumi, garnish with cress leaves and serve with fresh bread.

For 8 to share

Za'atar Red Mullet and Fennel Tzatziki Toasts

FOR THE TZATZIKI

- 1 large fennel bulb, trimmed and finely sliced
- 3 tablespoons olive oil
- 1 teaspoon fennel seeds
- 2 garlic cloves, crushed
- juice of 1 lemon
- 500g thick yoghurt or suzme (strained yoghurt, see instructions on p.183)

FOR THE MULLET

- 500g small red mullet fillets
- 3 tablespoons olive oil
- juice of 1 lemon
- 2 tablespoons za'atar

TO SERVE

- 8 small slices of chunky white bread or pitta bread
- za'atar (extra, to sprinkle)

TO MAKE THE TZATZIKI

In a pan, sauté the fennel in the olive oil on a low heat for 15–20 minutes, until creamy and caramelised. Remove from the heat and allow to cool. Meanwhile, toast the fennel seeds in a dry frying pan for 1 minute. Allow to cool, then finely grind the seeds using a mortar and pestle or a spice grinder. Combine the garlic, lemon juice, yoghurt or suzme and ground fennel seeds with the cooked fennel.

TO COOK THE MULLET

Brush the red mullet fillets with olive oil and cook in a hot dry pan, skin side down first, for 3–4 minutes, until golden on both sides. Drizzle with the lemon juice and sprinkle with the za'atar. Season to taste.

TO SERVE

Toast the bread, then spoon some fennel tzatziki on to the toast, top with the red mullet and sprinkle with za'atar.

For 8 to share

Lentil, Orzo and Pine Nut Pilaf with Saffron Onions

250g dried brown lentils

125g dried orzo or long-grain rice

2 tablespoons olive oil

1 red onion, finely sliced

small bunch of fresh oregano, leaves only

3 tablespoons pine nuts, toasted

FOR THE ONIONS

2 onions, finely sliced

2 tablespoons olive oil

1 teaspoon saffron threads

TO COOK THE PILAF

In a pan, cover the lentils with cold water and cook on a medium heat for about 20 minutes, or until the lentils are soft. Add the orzo and cook for a further 10 minutes, making sure the orzo is cooked through. Drain the liquid and keep the lentils and orzo warm. Heat the olive oil in a large frying pan, add the red onion, cooked lentils and orzo, and season to taste. Stir and cook for 5–6 minutes. Remove from the heat, then add the oregano and pine nuts.

TO COOK THE ONIONS

In a frying pan, on a medium heat, sauté the onions in the olive oil for about 15 minutes, until they are mushy and caramelised. Add the saffron and stir to combine.

Serve the pilaf hot, topped with the saffron onions.

For 8 to share

Chilled Carrot and Saffron Soup

1 onion, finely chopped
2 celery sticks, finely chopped
500g carrots, cubed
1 tablespoon olive oil
2–3 saffron threads
1.5 litres chicken stock
100ml coconut milk
50g pack of fresh coriander, finely chopped

In a large pan, sauté the onion, celery and carrots in the olive oil on a medium heat with the saffron for 5 minutes. Add the chicken stock, season to taste and bring to the boil. Reduce to a simmer, cover and cook for 15–20 minutes, until the carrots are soft. Remove from the heat and allow to cool, then blend in a food processor to a smooth purée. Return the soup to the pan, add the coconut milk, and simmer for 5 minutes. Allow to cool completely, then place in the refrigerator to chill.

Serve cold, sprinkled with coriander.

For 8 to share

Lemon Thyme Za'atar Fritto Misto

FOR THE LEMON THYME
ZA'ATAR

8 *fresh oregano sprigs, roughly torn, with flowers if possible*

8 *fresh lemon thyme sprigs, roughly torn*

2 *tablespoons sesame seeds*

2 *teaspoons ground sumac*

½ *teaspoon salt*

FOR THE FRITTO MISTO

1 *small fresh squid, approx. 400g, cut into pieces*

300g *fresh king prawns, de-shelled, tails intact*

400g *small red mullet fillets*

3 *lemons, cut into 1cm thick slices*

16 *lemon thyme sprigs*

2 *tablespoons cornflour*

vegetable oil, for deep-frying

TO SERVE

4 *lemons, cut into wedges*

TO MAKE THE LEMON THYME ZA'ATAR

Simply combine all the ingredients in a bowl.

TO MAKE THE FRITTO MISTO

Put the squid, king prawns and red mullet fillets into a large bowl along with the lemon slices and sprigs of lemon thyme. Sprinkle on two-thirds of the za'atar mixture, and gently toss to coat the seafood. Add the cornflour and again, gently toss. Place batches in a sieve and shake to rid the mixture of excess cornflour.

Heat the vegetable oil in a deep-fat fryer to 180°C. Carefully drop the coated seafood and lemon slices in small batches into the hot oil. Cook each batch for 1 minute, until golden. Remove with a slotted spoon and place on kitchen paper to drain.

TO SERVE

Pile the seafood on to a large platter, serve with the lemon wedges and sprinkle with the remaining za'atar.

For 8 to share

Fire & Noble Velvet

CHILLI AND CUMIN

The **chillies** that are used in the Eastern Mediterranean are not as fiery or as furious as those that are used in some other cuisines. Instead they are fragrant, with strong aromatic tones. Used sparingly, they can add sweet, smoky and nutty notes to a dish.

Aleppo, a town in the north of Syria, is famed throughout the region for its chilli production. Green or red – my preference is red – Aleppo chillies have an astonishing depth of flavour that is reminiscent of dried fruits or flowers. They add a caramelised flavour to chilli and za'atar chicken wings, and a sweet kick to cumin and chilli-crusted calamari. If you can't get hold of Aleppo chilli, which is usually sold as dried flakes, then use any mild and sweet variety of chilli.

Cumin is a native of the Eastern Mediterranean, where it thrives in hot arid conditions. It has been used in the cuisines of Syria and Persia, modern-day Iran, for at least 1,000 years. The seeds can be used either whole or ground; it doesn't have the fire of chilli but instead brings a whole labyrinth of elevating flavours, strong and warm, transforming dishes into something altogether more elegant.

The Greeks are so fond of cumin that they will keep a pot of ground cumin on the table to sprinkle on just about anything. It is great with meats, as part of a marinade, with pulses, or simply shaken on to breads and pastries before baking. Use fresh seeds whenever you can. Dry toast them, and then finely grind – that way you'll get the most out of the flavour.

Duck, Haloumi and Green Chilli Spring Rolls with Sweet Potato and Almond Skordalia

Skordalia is a Greek garlicky sauce or dip, usually made from either potatoes or bread. For a distinctive modern take on this traditional sauce I use sweet potato.

FOR THE SKORDALIA

- 1 large sweet potato, peeled and cubed
- 2 garlic cloves, crushed
- juice of 1 lemon
- 1 tablespoon ground almonds
- 5 tablespoons olive oil

FOR THE SPRING ROLLS

- 1 tablespoon olive oil
- 4 duck leg quarters, cut into small pieces
- ½ teaspoon ground cumin
- ½ small bunch fresh mint, chopped
- 2 garlic cloves, crushed
- 4 shallots, sliced
- 1 bay leaf
- 100ml chicken stock
- small bunch of fresh parsley, chopped
- 200g haloumi cheese, crumbled
- 3 small green chillies, de-seeded and finely sliced
- 12 large sheets of filo pastry (20cm × 20cm)
- 5–6 tablespoons melted butter
- 1 tablespoon za'atar

TO SERVE

- 1 teaspoon za'atar

TO MAKE THE SKORDALIA

Cook the sweet potato in boiling water for 20 minutes until soft. Drain and mash in a bowl, then add the garlic, lemon and ground almonds. While stirring, drizzle in the olive oil until well mixed in, and season to taste.

TO MAKE THE SPRING ROLLS

Preheat the oven to 180°C fan/gas mark 6.

Heat the olive oil in an ovenproof dish. Add the duck quarters, cumin, mint, garlic, bay leaf and shallots and cook for 5 minutes, until the meat is lightly browned. Add the stock, cover and cook in the oven for 45 minutes to 1 hour, until the duck is tender and cooked through. Remove the duck and place to one side until it is cool enough to handle, then pull the meat off the bones and shred it into a bowl, discarding the skin and bones. Mix in the parsley, haloumi cheese and green chillies. Add 6 tablespoons of the cooking juices.

Turn the oven up to 200°C fan/gas mark 7.

Place a large filo sheet on your work surface, brush with butter, then fold in two. Spoon some of the mixture in and gently spread along one edge. Fold in the sides to enclose the filling, then roll away from you to get a neat spring roll. Repeat the same with the remaining 11 filo sheets. Arrange the rolls on a baking tray seam side down, brush with the melted butter, and sprinkle with the za'atar. Bake in the oven for 5–6 minutes, until golden.

Serve the spring rolls hot, with the sweet potato and almond skordalia, and sprinkle the skordalia with some za'atar.

Makes 12

Chilli and Za'atar Chicken Wings

4 tablespoons olive oil

zest of 1 lemon

juice of ½ lemon

4 garlic cloves, crushed

1 tablespoon pomegranate molasses (see p. 175 for the recipe)

2 tablespoons za'atar

2 teaspoons Aleppo chilli flakes

24 chicken wings

1 tablespoon sesame seeds, toasted

4 HOURS IN ADVANCE

Combine the olive oil, lemon zest and juice, garlic, pomegranate molasses, za'atar and chilli flakes in a large bowl. Add the chicken wings and make sure they are well coated with the marinade. Cover and refrigerate for 4 hours.

Preheat the oven to 200°C fan/gas mark 7.

Arrange the marinated chicken wings on a large baking tray lined with foil. Sprinkle with the sesame seeds and cook in the oven for 25–30 minutes, turning halfway through to ensure they're evenly cooked.

Remove from the oven and serve hot or cold.

For 8 to share

Carrot, Cumin and Raisin Yoghurt Salad

The Russians have vodka, the Japanese have sake and the people of the Eastern
Mediterranean have raki. This mezze salad is the perfect accompaniment to raki,
or vice versa. Crunchy and creamy, it is reminiscent of coleslaw.

400g carrots, coarsely grated
1 tablespoon cumin seeds
2 tablespoons olive oil
200g thick yoghurt or suzme
(strained yoghurt, see
Instructions on p.183)
½ tablespoon mayonnaise
3 tablespoons raisins
2 garlic cloves, crushed

In a frying pan, sauté the grated carrot in the olive oil over a medium heat
for 2 minutes, until wilted but not brown. Place in a bowl and allow to cool
completely. Roast the cumin seeds for 2 minutes, then cool and finely grind.
Once the carrot has cooled, add the yoghurt or suzme, mayonnaise, raisins,
garlic and ground cumin. Stir well and season to taste.

For 8 to share

Chilli Chickpea Street Pilaf

One of the most common street foods in Turkey is a fluffy rice pilaf with chickpeas, known as nohutlu pilaf. It is claimed that this was one of the favourite dishes of the Conqueror, Sultan Mehmed II, and he ordered his chefs to add solid gold chickpeas to the real ones, so that his guests might share in the luck. I suggest that you use a can of chickpeas rather than solid gold, but this pilaf is still equally rich in flavour! The best rice to use is baldo, but Arborio or short-grain rice will work too.

1 onion, peeled and finely chopped

1 tablespoon clarified butter or ghee

250g baldo rice

200g tinned chickpeas, drained

500ml chicken or vegetable stock

¼ teaspoon chilli flakes

½ teaspoon paprika

In a large pan, sauté the onion in the butter over a medium heat for 2–3 minutes, until soft. Add the rice and stir well, ensuring all the rice grains are coated in the butter. Then add the chickpeas and stock. Cover the pan and cook on low to medium heat for 12–15 minutes, without stirring, until the stock is completely absorbed. The rice should be cooked but still have a little bite to it. Turn off the heat, cover the pan with a clean cloth, place a lid on top, and allow to rest for 15–20 minutes.

Serve with the chilli flakes and paprika sprinkled on top.

For 8 to share

Quick Cumin Börek

My friend Sevda introduced this easy dish to me. A quick version of an old favourite,
su börek, or water börek, is light, fast and delicious. Yufka pastry is ideal for this
recipe to work, as it's pre-cooked, but if you can't find it, use filo and add 10 minutes
cooking in a pre-heated 180°C oven.

3 eggs, beaten

50g melted butter

100ml water

3 sheets of yufka pastry

250g feta cheese, crumbled

small bunch of fresh parsley,
finely chopped

½ tablespoon cumin seeds

Combine the eggs, melted butter and water, and season to taste. Cut the
yufka pastry into small squares, approx. 2–3cm, and mix the pieces into
the egg mixture. In another bowl, mash the cheese with a fork and add
the parsley and cumin seeds.

Heat a large non-stick pan over a medium heat. Pour in half the egg and
yufka mixture, sprinkle with the cheese, then finish by pouring on the
remaining egg and yufka mixture. Cook on a low heat for 3–4 minutes, until
the underside is golden brown. Using a large plate, carefully turn out the
börek and return it to the frying pan to cook on the other side for a further
2–3 minutes.

Enjoy hot or cold.

For 8 to share

Wild Garlic and Cumin Choux Balls

My mother used to make these with either spinach or broad bean purée. In this recipe I've substituted wild garlic for spinach, but you can use almost any green leaf vegetable. Another difference from my mother's recipe is that I use panko breadcrumbs. These are readily available in most Asian shops, but if you can't get hold of them, toast ordinary breadcrumbs so they have a crunch to them.

1 teaspoon olive oil

150g wild garlic leaves, trimmed and chopped

200ml milk

200ml water

100g butter

200g plain flour

3 large eggs

125g feta cheese, crumbled

4–5 tablespoons panko breadcrumbs

1 teaspoon cumin seeds

vegetable oil, for deep-frying

TO SERVE

yoghurt, mint and garlic sauce (see p. 179 for the recipe)

2 HOURS IN ADVANCE

Heat the olive oil in a pan over a low heat. Add the wild garlic leaves and sauté for 2 minutes, then season to taste. Allow to cool sufficiently for you to handle. Squeeze out the excess water with your hands, then blend in a food processor to a purée and put to one side. Heat the milk, water and butter in a small non-stick saucepan. Slowly bring to a simmer, making sure the butter is melted. Sprinkle in the flour, stirring as you do so. Continue to cook and stir for 3–5 minutes, so that the mixture starts to come away from the side of the pan. When the mixture forms a ball in the centre of the pan, remove from the heat and, using a hand whisk if you have one or a fork if you don't, add the eggs one at a time, incorporating them into the mixture until it is soft and glossy. Now add the wild garlic purée and feta cheese, and mix again until well combined. Season and mix again. Place the mixture in a bowl, cover and refrigerate for a couple of hours.

TO COOK THE CHOUX BALLS

Mix the panko breadcrumbs and cumin in a shallow dish. Shape the choux mixture into 20 small balls – about the size of golf balls – and roll each ball in the panko and cumin. Heat the vegetable oil in a deep-fat fryer to 180°C. Drop the coated balls into the hot oil and fry for 3–4 minutes, until golden, and when they float to the top remove them with a slotted wooden spoon and drain on kitchen paper.

Serve with Yoghurt, Mint and Garlic Sauce.

Makes 20

Pumpkin Skordalia with Pine Nut and Nigella Seed Dukkah

FOR THE SKORDALIA

2 medium baking potatoes

500g pumpkin, peeled, de-seeded and cubed

3 tablespoons olive oil

10 sage leaves

200g pine nuts, finely ground

4 garlic cloves, crushed

1 tablespoon lemon juice

FOR THE DUKKAH

100g pine nuts

2 tablespoons dried coconut, grated

2 tablespoons coriander seeds

2 tablespoons cumin seeds

2 tablespoons nigella seeds

½ teaspoon salt

½ teaspoon crushed black pepper

TO SERVE

small bowl of olive oil

fresh crusty bread

1 HOUR IN ADVANCE

Preheat the oven to 180°C fan/gas mark 6 one hour in advance.

Place the baking potatoes in the oven and cook for 1–1½ hours (depending on size), until soft right through. Remove and allow to cool. Meanwhile, place the pumpkin cubes on a baking tray and drizzle with the olive oil. Season and sprinkle with the sage leaves. Roast for approximately 50 minutes, or until the pumpkin is well cooked. Set aside the oil

TO PREPARE THE SKORDALIA

While the roasted pumpkin is still hot, place it in a food processor along with the cooking juices and sage leaves. Blend to a smooth purée. Scoop the cooked flesh from the baked potatoes and add it to the puréed pumpkin. Blend again, then add the ground pine nuts, garlic, lemon juice and the olive oil in which you roasted the pumpkin. Blend until well combined. Season and place in a serving dish.

TO MAKE THE DUKKAH

In a dry frying pan, toast the pine nuts for 1–2 minutes, shaking the pan to toast evenly, until they are lightly golden in colour. Turn out on to a board and roughly chop. Using the same pan, toast the coconut along with the coriander, cumin and nigella seeds for 1–2 minutes, until you can smell the fragrant aroma. Remove and cool, then coarsely grind the mixture and combine in a serving bowl with the toasted pine nuts, salt and black pepper.

TO SERVE

Serve the pumpkin skordalia and the dukkah in two separate bowls, accompanied by a small bowl of olive oil and plenty of crusty bread. Enjoy by dipping the bread in the oil, then into the dukkah, and finally topping with a generous helping of the pumpkin skordalia.

For 8 to share

Courgette and Cumin Falafel

1 tablespoon olive oil

1 large onion, finely chopped

2 teaspoons ground cumin

¼ teaspoon ground allspice

220ml milk

100g chickpea flour

3 tablespoons tinned chickpeas, drained

3 tablespoons lemon juice

4 small to medium courgettes, grated and squeezed dry

vegetable oil, for deep-frying

2 HOURS IN ADVANCE

Heat 1 tablespoon of the olive oil and sauté the onion, cumin and allspice for 3–4 minutes. Remove and transfer to a bowl.

In a medium non-stick pan, bring the milk to the boil then reduce to a simmer. Little by little, whisk in the chickpea flour until you have a smooth paste. Keep the mixture moving to avoid lumps. Season then add the remaining olive oil and cook on a low heat for 8 minutes, stirring all the time with a wooden spoon. Like choux pastry, the mixture will come away from the sides of the pan and work into a ball, solidifying as it is heated.

Cool the ball of paste, then mix in the sautéed onions, chickpeas, lemon juice and grated courgettes. Using your hands, mould the mixture into small balls and arrange on a tray. Chill in the fridge for a couple of hours.

TO COOK THE FALAFEL

Heat some oil in a pan, enough to cover the falafel balls, and heat until very hot. Carefully place the falafel, a few at a time, into the oil and cook for 3–4 minutes, until golden brown. Remove with a slotted spoon and place on kitchen paper to drain.

Delicious served hot with Carrot, Cumin and Yoghurt Salad, and Aleppo-style Cumin Scented Baba Ganoush.

For 8 to share

Cumin and Chilli-Crusted Calamari with Tahini and Chilli Mayonnaise

FOR THE TAHINI AND CHILLI MAYONNAISE

3 egg yolks

150g groundnut oil

150g olive oil

1 tablespoon tahini

juice of ½ lemon

½ tablespoon mild chilli flakes

FOR THE CALAMARI

1 fresh medium-sized squid, approx. 800g

4 tablespoons plain flour

1 teaspoon mild chilli flakes

1 tablespoon ground cumin

¼ teaspoon salt

¼ teaspoon pepper

vegetable oil, for deep-frying

TO MAKE THE MAYONNAISE

Whisk the egg yolks and slowly drizzle in the oils, until you get a mayo-like consistency. Add tahini and lemon, and mix. Season and sprinkle with the chilli flakes.

TO COOK THE CALAMARI

Slice the squid into 1cm rings and dry with kitchen paper.

Combine the flour, chilli flakes, cumin, salt and pepper in a bowl and coat the squid rings in the mixture, a few at a time. Put to one side, ready to fry.

Heat the vegetable oil in a deep-fat fryer to 180°C. Gently drop the coated squid rings, a few at a time, into the hot oil and cook for 1 minute, until golden brown. Remove with a slotted wooden spoon and place on kitchen paper to drain. It's best to avoid cooking too many rings at once, as it reduces the temperature of the oil and the calamari won't crisp up as well.

Serve hot, with the tahini and chilli mayonnaise.

For 8 to share

Suzme and Chilli Marinated Chicken Shawarma with Aubergine and Red Pepper Salad

8 chicken thighs

FOR THE MARINADE

3 tablespoons thick yoghurt or suzme (strained yoghurt, see instructions on p.183)

4 garlic cloves, crushed

6 tablespoons olive oil

zest and juice of 2 lemons

2 tablespoons white wine vinegar

2 tablespoons chilli sauce

1 tablespoon Aleppo chilli flakes (or any mild red chilli flakes)

2 teaspoons cinnamon

1 teaspoon fresh nutmeg, grated

1 teaspoon ground cardamom

FOR THE SALAD

2 medium aubergines

3 red peppers

2 garlic cloves, crushed

1 ripe tomato, finely chopped

3 tablespoons olive oil

TO SERVE

50g walnuts, roughly chopped

50g pack of fresh coriander, finely sliced

TO MAKE THE MARINADE

Combine all the marinade ingredients in a bowl and season to taste. Add the chicken, stir to coat, and leave in a covered bowl in the fridge to marinate for 12 hours.

TO PREPARE THE SALAD

Preheat the oven to 200°C fan/gas mark 7.

Arrange the whole aubergines and peppers on an oven tray and roast for 20–30 minutes, turning so that all the skin is charred. Take out of the oven and allow to cool. Remove the skin from the aubergines and discard. Put the aubergine flesh in a food processor and blend until you have a smooth purée. Spoon into a separate bowl.

Remove the skin from the peppers, then de-seed and finely chop them. Add the chopped pepper to the aubergine purée along with the garlic, tomato and olive oil. Season to taste.

Discarding the marinade, place the chicken under a hot grill for approx. 20–30 minutes until cooked right through, turning occasionally.

To serve, spoon the aubergine and pepper salad on to the plates and sprinkle with the walnuts and coriander. Shred the chicken, discarding the skin and bones, and layer on top of the salad. This is good hot or cold.

For 8 to share

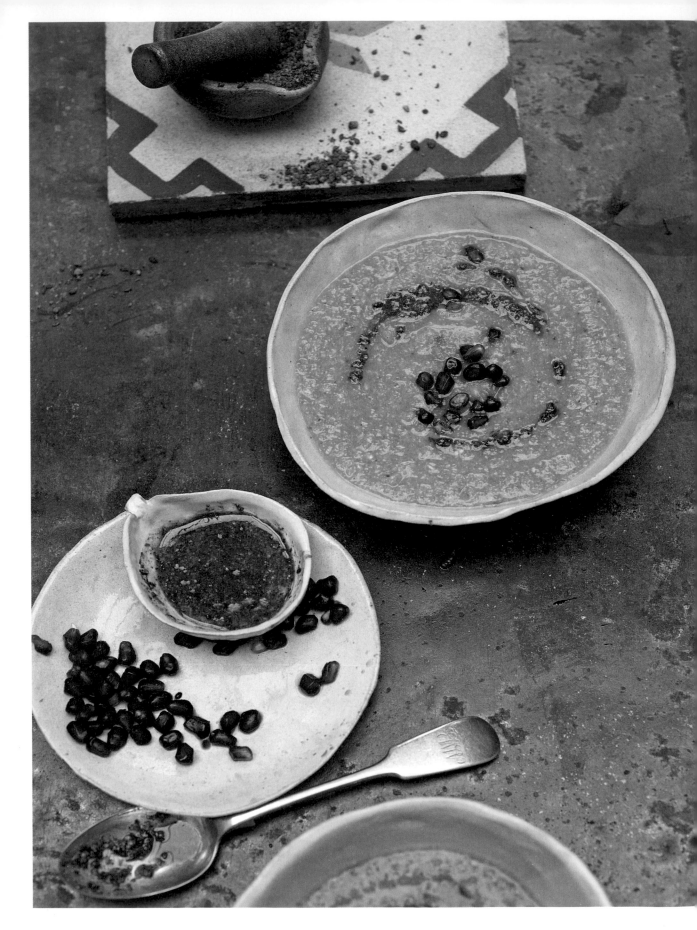

Roast Pumpkin and Almond Soup
with Almond and Cumin Dukkah

Dukkah is an Egyptian spice and nut blend that has a fantastic crunchy texture. Here I've mixed the dukkah with olive oil so that it blends deliciously with this comforting autumnal soup.

FOR THE DUKKAH

- 50g whole almonds, toasted
- 1 tablespoon coriander seeds, toasted
- ½ tablespoon cumin seeds, toasted
- ¼ tablespoon fennel seeds, toasted
- 6 tablespoons olive oil

FOR THE SOUP

- 1kg pumpkin or squash, peeled, de-seeded and cubed
- 8 fresh sage leaves, finely chopped
- 2 onions, quartered
- 6 garlic cloves
- 4 tablespoons olive oil
- 800ml chicken stock
- 100g ground almonds

TO SERVE

- 3 tablespoons pomegranate seeds

TO MAKE THE DUKKAH

Place all the ingredients in a food processor and blend until well combined. Transfer to a small bowl.

TO MAKE THE SOUP

Preheat the oven to 180°C fan/gas mark 6.

Spread the pumpkin, sage, onions and whole garlic cloves on a roasting tray and drizzle with the olive oil. Season to taste and cook in the oven for 30–35 minutes, until the pumpkin is soft. Remove from oven and allow to cool a little.

Using a food processor, blend to a purée, adding a little of the chicken stock to ease the process. Tip the pumpkin purée into a saucepan and add the rest of the stock. Simmer for 20 minutes, stirring from time to time to ensure a smooth consistency. Finally, add the ground almonds and combine well.

TO SERVE

Drizzle the soup with the almond dukkah and sprinkle with pomegranate seeds.

For 6 to share

Fava Bean and Green Chilli Falafel with Yoghurt and Tahini Sauce

Falafel plays a major role in every Eastern Mediterranean cuisine. Shaped into balls and deep-fried, it is made from fava beans (dried broad beans) or chickpeas, or a combination of both. Serve as a mezze dish with this yoghurt and tahini sauce, or as an accompaniment to lamb or spinach dishes.

FOR THE SAUCE

100ml plain yoghurt

2 tablespoons tahini

2 garlic cloves, crushed

juice of 1 lemon

50ml water

FOR THE FALAFEL

225g dried fava beans, soaked overnight

4 spring onions, chopped

4 garlic cloves, crushed

small bunch of fresh parsley, chopped

small bunch of fresh mint, chopped

1 teaspoon cumin seeds, toasted and crushed

1 small green chilli, de-seeded and finely chopped

1 teaspoon ground coriander

1½ teuspoons baking powder

vegetable oil, for deep-frying

TO SERVE

¼ teaspoon cracked black pepper

½ teaspoon sea salt flakes

TO MAKE THE SAUCE

Combine all the ingredients and season to taste.

TO MAKE THE FALAFEL

Drain the fava beans and place two thirds of them in a saucepan with fresh cold water. Bring to the boil and simmer for 20 minutes, until tender. Drain and allow to cool slightly. Meanwhile, place the remaining uncooked beans in a food processor and blend until smooth, then remove them to a bowl. Put the cooked beans into the processor and blend to a purée, then spoon into a separate mixing bowl. Add the spring onions, garlic, parsley, mint, cumin, green chilli, coriander and baking powder, and season. Finally, add the puréed uncooked beans to the mixture.

Shape the falafel mixture into walnut-sized balls and flatten into discs, about 2cm thick. Heat the vegetable oil in a deep frying pan until very hot. Carefully cook 3 falafel at a time for 6–8 minutes, turning until evenly browned. Remove with a slotted wooden spoon and drain on kitchen paper.

TO SERVE

Arrange the warm falafel on a serving plate and drizzle over the yoghurt and tahini sauce. Sprinkle with the black pepper and sea salt.

For 8 to share

Chicken Stuffed Yoghurt and Cumin Pastry Börek

FOR THE PASTRY

50g yoghurt

60g melted butter (plus 20g extra, for brushing)

1 small egg, beaten

165g self-raising flour

1 teaspoon cumin seeds

flour, for rolling

1 egg yolk, for brushing

FOR THE FILLING

2 shallots, finely chopped

1 small garlic clove, crushed

½ teaspoon ground cumin

¼ teaspoon paprika

¼ teaspoon chilli flakes

1 skinless chicken breast, finely chopped

1 tablespoon olive oil

small bunch of fresh mint, finely chopped

1 HOUR IN ADVANCE

Combine the yoghurt, melted butter, egg, flour and cumin seeds in a bowl until you have a soft, pliable dough. Cover and rest in the fridge for 1 hour.

TO MAKE THE FILLING

In a non-stick pan, sauté the shallots, garlic, spices and chicken in the olive oil on a high heat for 3–5 minutes, until the chicken is well cooked. Remove from the heat and allow to cool, then add the mint and seasoning to taste.

Preheat the oven to 160°C fan/gas mark 4.

Place the dough on a floured surface and roll out to about 25 × 25cm. Brush with a little of the extra melted butter and fold in half. Repeat this so that you have a small square. Brush once more, then cut the pastry in two and roll each piece on a floured surface to make 2 rectangles about 3mm thick. Split the filling between the pastry rectangles and spread along the length of the pastry, then fold each one over, sealing the edges and ends with a little water to make 2 sausages.

Arrange the böreks on a lightly oiled baking tray and brush with the egg yolk. Bake in the oven for 20–25 minutes, until golden brown.

Serve warm or cold, cut into bite-sized pieces.

For 8 to share

Lamb Moussaka Rolls

2 large aubergines

6 tablespoons olive oil, for brushing

FOR THE FILLING

1 small onion, finely chopped

1 tablespoon olive oil

400g ground lamb

2 large tomatoes, finely chopped

1 teaspoon ground cumin

½ teaspoon paprika

½ teaspoon mild chilli powder

½ teaspoon oregano

small bunch of fresh parsley, leaves only, finely chopped

2 small tomatoes, thinly sliced

50g Parmesan cheese, grated

TO SERVE

300g thick yoghurt or suzme (strained yoghurt, see instructions on p.183)

1 teaspoon nigella seeds

TO COOK THE AUBERGINES

Preheat the oven to 180°C fan/gas mark 6.

Thinly slice the aubergines lengthways, about ½cm in thickness. You should have 8–10 slices. Arrange the slices on a baking tray and brush generously with olive oil. Place in the oven and roast for 10 minutes, until soft and golden. Remove from the oven and allow to cool.

TO MAKE THE FILLING

In a large frying pan, sauté the onion in the olive oil for 2 minutes, until soft. Add the lamb and cook for a further 4–5 minutes, stirring to brown on all sides. Add the tomatoes, cumin, paprika, chilli and oregano, and season to taste. Simmer for 10 minutes, until any liquid has mostly evaporated and the mixture is thick. Remove from the heat, stir in the fresh parsley and allow to cool.

TO MAKE THE ROLLS

Preheat the grill to medium/high.

Take a cooled slice of aubergine, place a spoonful of the filling on one end, and carefully roll it up. Arrange the aubergine rolls seam side down on a grill pan. Place a slice of tomato, or half a slice if that fits better, on top of each roll, and sprinkle with the Parmesan. Grill for about 2 minutes, until the cheese is golden.

TO SERVE

Place the yoghurt or suzme in a bowl and sprinkle with the nigella seeds. Serve with the moussaka rolls, straight from the grill.

For 8 to share

Aleppo-Style Cumin Scented Baba Ghanoush

In Syria there are as many recipes for baba ghanoush as there are people making it. Best made as they do in Aleppo, with plenty of cumin, or as they do in Damascus, without cumin but with lots of fruity olive oil? More than one family has been known to fall out over such matters. I prefer the Aleppo version, so here it is.

2 large aubergines

1 tablespoon ground cumin

1 small green pepper, de-seeded and finely chopped

1 small onion, finely chopped

1 ripe tomato, finely chopped

2 garlic cloves, crushed

small bunch of fresh parsley, finely chopped

juice of 1 lemon

2 tablespoons pomegranate molasses (see p. 175 for the recipe)

50g walnuts, roughly chopped

Place the aubergines directly on a naked gas flame (or the electric ring if you are using electric) and, taking care, cook on a medium heat for 10–12 minutes, turning occasionally, so that the aubergines are chargrilled evenly. The skin will blacken and start blistering and the aubergines will become soft, not to mention the fact that your kitchen will be filled with a wonderful smell. Alternatively, you can bake the aubergines in the oven for 20 minutes at 200°C fan/gas mark 7, but the flavour won't be quite the same. Once cooked, place the aubergines in a strong plastic bag and allow them to sweat for around 20 minutes, which will make them easier to peel.

Peel and chop the aubergines, discarding any uncooked pieces you might find. Press the chopped flesh into a sieve. Over a bowl, press down gently to get out as much liquid as possible. (Never be tempted to purée the aubergines.) Discard the liquid. Tip the aubergine into a large bowl and, using a fork, combine with the cumin, pepper, onion, tomato, garlic, parsley and lemon juice. Season to taste.

Serve drizzled with the pomegranate molasses and sprinkled with the chopped walnuts.

For 6 to share

Sea Bass and Prawn Mini Kebabs with Tahini and Chilli Sauce

FOR THE SAUCE

- 2 tablespoons tahini
- 1 tablespoon mild chilli sauce
- zest and juice of 1 small lemon
- ½ large garlic clove, crushed
- 1 tablespoon olive oil
- 1 teaspoon sesame seeds, toasted
- 80ml water

FOR THE KEBABS

- 2 sea bass fillets, approx. 500g each, skins removed
- 300g raw king prawns, shells and tails removed
- juice of 1 lemon
- small bunch of fresh coriander, finely chopped
- ¼ teaspoon ground cardamom
- 1 large red chilli, de-seeded and finely chopped
- 2 egg yolks

TO MAKE THE SAUCE

Simply combine all the ingredients until you get a smooth sauce and season to taste. Add a little more water if needed to get a thinner sauce.

TO COOK THE KEBABS

Preheat the grill to medium/high.

Dice the sea bass very finely, until almost minced. Cube the prawns and mix together with the sea bass in a bowl. Add the lemon, coriander, cardamom and chilli, then add the egg yolks. Mix well and season to taste. Using your hands, shape into small cocktail-sausage size kebabs. Grill for 3 minutes on each side, until golden.

Serve hot, with the tahini and chilli sauce.

For 8 to share

Chickpea and Cumin Kofte with Tahini and Lemon Sauce

FOR THE KOFTE

200g dried chickpeas, soaked overnight

1 large onion, grated

1 ripe tomato, cubed

small bunch of fresh mint, leaves only, finely chopped

2 teaspoons ground cumin

1 tablespoon plain flour (plus 3 tablespoons extra, for dusting)

2 tablespoons vegetable oil, for frying

FOR THE SAUCE

3 tablespoons tahini

juice of 1 small lemon

½ tablespoon sumac

3 tablespoons olive oil

100ml water

TO MAKE THE KOFTE

Drain the chickpeas and place in a saucepan. Cover with cold water and bring to the boil, then reduce to a simmer and cook for 1 hour or until soft. Drain again then place in a food processor, blending until you have a coarse purée.

Tip the chickpea purée into a bowl and add the onion, tomato, mint and cumin. Season to taste and work in the tablespoon of flour until you have a pliable mixture. Using your hands, shape into small patties and dust with the extra flour.

Heat the vegetable oil in a non-stick pan and pan-fry the kofte, a few at a time, on a medium to high heat for roughly 1 minute on each side, until golden. Remove and place on kitchen paper to drain.

TO MAKE THE SAUCE

Combine the tahini, lemon and sumac in a bowl, adding 2 tablespoons of water at a time to thin the sauce a little. Finally, add the olive oil and sprinkle with sumac. Serve with the hot kofte.

For 8 to share

Spiced Pork and Cumin Sausages with Fennel and Preserved Lemon Salad

500g   ground pork

2   garlic cloves, crushed

1½   teaspoons ground cumin

¼   teaspoon ground nutmeg

¼   teaspoon ground cinnamon

½   teaspoon ground coriander

1   teaspoon mint

1   teaspoon oregano

½   teaspoon chilli flakes

1   teaspoon paprika

100ml   water

FOR THE SALAD

2   small fennel bulbs, sliced paper-thin

1   preserved lemon, pulp removed, rind finely sliced

10   green olives, chopped

small bunch of fresh coriander, finely chopped

3   tablespoons olive oil

3   tablespoons lemon juice

TO SERVE

3–4   tablespoons thick yoghurt or suzme (strained yoghurt, see instructions on p. 183)

a few preserved green chillis

flatbread

TO MAKE THE SAUSAGES

Combine all the ingredients together, holding back some of the water until the mixture is moist but not too sticky. Season to taste, mix well, then using your hands shape into 16 small sausages. Cook at a high heat on a griddle pan or under the grill for 3–5 minutes on each side, until golden and cooked all the way through.

TO MAKE THE SALAD

Mix together the fennel, preserved lemon rind, olives and coriander. Season to taste, then drizzle with the olive oil and lemon juice.

TO SERVE

Arrange the pork and cumin sausages on flatbread with the salad around it and a green chilli and the yoghurt or suzme drizzled on top.

Makes 16

Summer Squash, Feta and Cumin Kofte with Wild Garlic Tzatziki

Tzatziki is normally made with cucumbers – this is a modern take on that theme. If you can't get hold of wild garlic, then use watercress or spinach instead.

FOR THE TZATZIKI

- 300g wild garlic leaves, chopped
- 1 teaspoon olive oil
- 300ml thick yoghurt or suzme (strained yoghurt, see instructions on p.183)
- 2 teaspoons olive oil (extra)

FOR THE KOFTE

- 800g summer squash, peeled and grated
- 150g wild garlic leaves, chopped
- 250g feta cheese, crumbled
- 4 spring onions, finely chopped
- 50g pack of fresh thyme, leaves only, finely chopped
- 2 large eggs, beaten
- 1 teaspoon ground cumin
- 4 tablespoons breadcrumbs
- 3 tablespoons flour, for dusting
- 2–4 tablespoons olive oil, for frying

TO SERVE

- 1 tablespoon pine nuts, toasted

TO MAKE THE TZATZIKI

In a pan, sauté the chopped wild garlic leaves in the olive oil on a medium heat for 1 minute. Place the sautéed garlic in a bowl and allow to cool completely. Once cool, combine with the yoghurt and extra olive oil. Leave to chill in the refrigerator.

TO COOK THE KOFTE

In a large bowl, combine the squash, wild garlic, feta, onions, thyme, eggs, cumin and breadcrumbs. Season to taste and refrigerate for 30 minutes. When ready to cook, shape into 25 small balls and dust with the flour.

Heat the olive oil in a non-stick pan and pan-fry the kofte on a medium to high heat for 5–6 minutes.

TO SERVE

Enjoy the kofte hot or cold, with the chilled tzatziki, sprinkled with toasted pine nuts.

Makes 25

Cumin Marinated Mackerel Fillets with Cumin and Lemon Thyme-Infused Shallot Purée

FOR THE MACKEREL

1 tablespoon ground cumin

4 tablespoons olive oil (plus extra, for brushing)

zest and juice of 1 lemon

12 small mackerel fillets

FOR THE PURÉE

16 shallots, sliced

1 teaspoon cumin seeds

1 tablespoon olive oil

100ml chicken stock

4 tablespoons double cream

50g pack of fresh lemon thyme, finely chopped

TO SERVE

1 teaspoon cumin seeds, toasted

1 teaspoon sumac

4 HOURS IN ADVANCE

Prepare the marinade by combining the cumin, olive oil, lemon juice and zest in a bowl. Season to taste and add the mackerel fillets. Coat them well, then cover the bowl and leave to marinate in the fridge for at least 4 hours.

TO MAKE THE PURÉE

In a pan, sauté the shallots and cumin seeds in the olive oil on a medium heat for about 8 minutes, until golden and soft. Add the chicken stock, turn the heat up a little and cook until almost all the liquid has evaporated. Add the double cream and simmer for a few minutes, again until almost all the liquid has evaporated. Allow to cool a little before seasoning and blending to a purée. Finally, stir in the lemon thyme.

TO COOK THE MACKEREL

Heat a griddle pan or heavy frying pan until it is very hot. Brush the mackerel fillets on both sides with olive oil and cook for 2 minutes on each side, skin side down first.

TO SERVE

Spoon some of the cumin and lemon thyme-infused shallot purée on to each plate and top with 2 mackerel fillets. Sprinkle with some cumin seeds and sumac and serve hot.

For 6 to share

Chilli-Scented King Prawn and Feta Guvech

This dish brings memories of my father flooding back. Every weekend he would make one form of guvech or another. Vegetable guvech was his favourite and he kept an old earthenware pot for that sole purpose. Somewhere over the years the pot disappeared or was broken and now, whenever I am in Istanbul, I search through the bric-a-brac shops in the hope that I may find a similar one and thereby reproduce something even half as good as my father would make in his. Simple, but extremely tasty, you can also make this dish using haloumi cheese.

6 spring onions, cut into 2cm pieces

2 garlic cloves

2cm fresh ginger, peeled and grated

½ teaspoon Aleppo chilli flakes (or any mild chilli pepper flakes)

2 ripe tomatoes, cubed

1 tablespoon pomegranate molasses (see p.175 for the recipe)

3 tablespoons olive oil

½ small bunch of oregano, finely chopped

12 king prawns, peeled and de-veined

60g feta cheese, crumbled

2 tablespoons olive oil (extra)

Preheat the oven to 200°C fan/gas mark 7.

In a medium-sized casserole dish, saute the onions, ginger, garlic, chilli, tomatoes and pomegranate molasses in the olive oil on a medium heat for 10 minutes. Stir in the oregano and season to taste.

Top the casserole with the prawns and cover with the crumbled feta. Drizzle with the extra olive oil and cook in the oven for 10–12 minutes, until the cheese is golden and the prawns are cooked through.

Delicious served simply with fresh crusty bread.

For 4 to share

Spicy Cumin Mussels with Pesto and Lemon-Infused Mascarpone

FOR THE MUSSELS

1kg   fresh mussels, scrubbed and beards removed

3   tablespoons olive oil

2   garlic cloves

½   teaspoon ground cumin

¼   teaspoon chilli flakes

1   tomato, finely cubed

100ml   dry white wine

400ml   chicken stock

FOR THE MASCARPONE

300g   mascarpone cheese

2   tablespoons fresh pesto (see p.175 for the recipe)

2   tablespoons lemon juice

zest of 1 lemon

3–4   tablespoons olive oil

TO SERVE

small bunch of fresh basil, leaves only

fresh, crusty bread

TO COOK THE MUSSELS

Ensure that the mussels are really well washed. Discard any that are already open. In a large saucepan heat the olive oil with the garlic, cumin, chilli and tomato. Stir for 1–2 minutes and when really hot, tip in the washed mussels. Add the wine and stock. Cover and cook for 5 minutes, shaking the pan from time to time. Take off the heat and discard any mussels that haven't opened.

Preheat the grill to high.

Arrange the opened, cooked mussels on a deep, heatproof platter (one that will fit under your grill) and save 4 tablespoons of the cooking liquid for the mascarpone.

TO PREPARE THE MASCARPONE

Tip all the ingredients, aside from the oil, into a bowl along with the 4 tablespoons of cooking liquid saved from the poached mussels. Stir thoroughly to combine, season to taste, then pour the mixture over the cooked mussels. Drizzle with the olive oil and place under the hot grill for 2 minutes.

Serve hot, scattered with basil leaves and some fresh, crusty bread on the side to soak up the delicious juices.

For 8 to share

Cumin-Spiced Rabbit with Hazelnut Skordalia Sauce

FOR THE RABBIT

1 tablespoon ground allspice

½ teaspoon ground cloves

½ teaspoon ground black pepper

¼ teaspoon ground nutmeg

1 tablespoon ground cumin

2 × 1kg rabbits, jointed and cut into small pieces

4 tablespoons olive oil

2 bay leaves

500ml chicken stock

FOR THE SKORDALIA

2 slices of white bread, crusts removed

80g ground hazelnuts

80g ground almonds

5 garlic cloves

200ml olive oil

juice of 1 lemon

50–100ml chicken stock (optional)

TO SERVE

150g Parmesan cheese, grated

TO COOK THE RABBIT

Preheat the oven to 180°C fan/gas mark 6.

Mix the 5 spices together in a bowl and add the rabbit pieces, making sure they are well coated. In a large casserole dish, heat the olive oil to a high heat. Add the bay leaves and the coated rabbit pieces and cook for 5 minutes, until the rabbit is evenly browned. Add the chicken stock, cover and place in the oven for 45–50 minutes, until the meat is tender. Remove from the oven and keep warm.

TO MAKE THE SKORDALIA

Soak the bread in a bowl of water for a few seconds. Squeeze dry and place in a food processor with the hazelnuts, almonds and garlic. Blend while drizzling in the olive oil, until you have a smooth purée-like consistency. Add the lemon juice and season to taste. If you find that this is too thick a consistency for your liking, add 50–100ml of hot stock to thin a little.

Preheat the grill to high.

Arrange the rabbit pieces in an ovenproof dish, spoon over the sauce and top with the grated cheese. Grill for a few minutes until very lightly browned, and serve immediately.

For 8 to share

Spiced Duck Rillette with Courgette and Chilli Pesto

FOR THE DUCK

150ml thick yoghurt or suzme (strained yoghurt, see instructions on p. 183)

4 tablespoons white wine vinegar

5 tablespoons olive oil

zest of 2 large oranges

½ teaspoon ground cardamom

2 teaspoons baharat (see p. 173 for the recipe)

4 duck leg quarters

2 tablespoons olive oil (extra)

100ml water

FOR THE PESTO

2 medium courgettes

1 tablespoon olive oil, for brushing

2 green chillies, de-seeded and finely chopped

2 tablespoons pine nuts, toasted and chopped

3 garlic cloves, crushed

30g Parmesan cheese, grated

15 basil leaves, finely chopped

3 tablespoons olive oil (extra)

TO SERVE

Turkish bread, or flatbread

1 DAY IN ADVANCE

Combine the yoghurt or suzme, white wine vinegar, olive oil, orange zest, cardamom and baharat in a large bowl. Add the duck legs, coat well, cover and leave to marinate overnight in the fridge.

TO COOK THE DUCK

Preheat the oven to 180°C fan/gas mark 6.

Remove the duck legs from the marinade. In a non-stick, ovenproof pan, brown the duck legs in the extra olive oil on a high heat for 5–6 minutes, turning halfway through. Add the water, cover with foil and cook in the oven for 1 hour. Remove the foil and cook for a further 20 minutes.

TO MAKE THE PESTO

While the duck is cooking, preheat the grill to high. Cut the courgettes lengthways, in slices about 5mm thick, and lightly brush the slices with olive oil and grill for 1–2 minutes on each side, until golden. Allow to cool a little before finely chopping the cooked courgette. Place in a bowl and combine with the chillies, pine nuts, garlic, Parmesan, basil and olive oil. Season to taste.

TO SERVE

Once the duck has cooked, remove it from the oven and allow to cool enough to handle. Shred the meat and discard the skin (if you prefer). Gently toast the bread, lightly brushing with olive oil if you wish. Then place some warm sliced duck with a dollop of courgette and green chilli pesto on each flatbread.

For 8 to share

Cumin-Scented Jerusalem Artichoke Soup with Fresh Crab

2 garlic cloves, crushed

30g butter

1 tablespoon olive oil

500g Jerusalem artichokes, peeled and chopped

1 large potato, peeled and cubed

1 tablespoon cumin seeds, toasted

500ml chicken stock (vegetable stock may be used as a substitute)

300ml double cream

200g fresh white crabmeat, cooked

TO SERVE

1 punnet of basil cress (or small bunch of fresh basil)

2 very ripe tomatoes, finely cubed

In a large saucepan, sauté the garlic in the butter and olive oil for 1 minute on a medium heat. Add the Jerusalem artichokes and potato and continue to cook, stirring all the time, for a further 5 minutes. Add the cumin and the stock and bring to the boil. Reduce to a simmer and cook for 10–15 minutes, until the artichokes are soft. Remove from the heat and allow to cool a little before blending to a purée in a food processor. Add the cream and return to the saucepan to warm through and season to taste.

Serve in small bowls, topped with the cooked crabmeat and sprinkled with some basil cress leaves and the cubed tomato.

For 8 to share

Spaghetti with Octopus and Aleppo Chilli Sauce

500g octopus, poached
      (see instructions on p. 103)

3 shallots, finely chopped

3 tablespoons olive oil

2 garlic cloves, crushed

½ teaspoon Aleppo chilli flakes

150ml dry white wine

6 large tomatoes, skinned and cubed

400g dried spaghetti

TO SERVE

small bunch of fresh oregano, leaves only

TO MAKE THE SAUCE

Remove and discard the octopus head, then slice the body and tentacles into 2cm pieces. In a saucepan, gently sauté the shallots in the olive oil on a low heat for 10 minutes, until soft and translucent. Stir in the garlic and chilli, and season to taste. Finally, add the wine, tomatoes and the octopus slices. Gently simmer on a low heat for 20–25 minutes, until the octopus is very soft and tender.

Meanwhile, cook the spaghetti according to the packet instructions.

TO SERVE

Toss the cooked spaghetti with the octopus sauce and garnish with the oregano.

For 8 to share

Cumin-Scented Chicken Shawarma Caesar-style Salad

You might not think you know what shawarma is, but you do! Shawarma, or chevirme, comes from the Turkish meaning 'turning', hence shawarma is the revolving meat on a vertical spit cooker seen in just about every Turkish restaurant and takeaway. Sliced and served with salad in a flatbread, shawarma is the best-loved fast food of the Eastern Mediterranean.

FOR THE CHICKEN

- 6 garlic cloves, crushed
- juice of 2 lemons
- 2 bay leaves
- 2 tablespoons ground cumin
- 1 teaspoon ground cardamom
- ¼ teaspoon ground cloves
- 1 cinnamon stick, broken
- ½ teaspoon mild chilli powder
- 6 chicken breasts, skin removed

FOR THE DRESSING

- 4 tablespoons low-fat mayonnaise
- 2 garlic cloves, crushed
- 1 tablespoon tahini
- juice of 1 small lemon
- 3 tablespoons olive oil
- 100g Parmesan cheese, finely grated

FOR THE SALAD

- 6 baby gem lettuces, washed and broken into pieces

1 DAY IN ADVANCE

Combine the crushed garlic, lemon juice, bay leaves, cumin, cardamom, cloves, cinnamon and chilli in a large bowl. Season, then add the chicken breasts. Coat well, cover and refrigerate overnight.

TO COOK THE CHICKEN

Remove the chicken from the marinade and cook on a griddle pan, or under a medium/high grill, for about 15 minutes, turning to make sure it is evenly cooked all the way through. Once cooked, cut into slices.

TO MAKE THE SALAD

Combine all the dressing ingredients and toss with the leaves. Arrange the leaves topped with the chicken shawarma.

For 8 to share

Purple Citrus & Summer Breeze

SUMAC AND FRESH HERBS

I absolutely love the citrusy **sumac**. Whole, crushed or ground, I don't care; it's my favourite friend in the kitchen. Sumac is made from the clusters of small crimson or purple berries from the bush of the same name. It is extremely popular in Turkish and Lebanese cuisine, where it is considered an absolute essential and is even used where others might add lemon juice or vinegar. Its versatility is phenomenal. It's fantastic simply rubbed on to kebabs and chicken; sprinkled on fish and vegetables; in sauces, marinades and salads; to flavour butter; and to enhance the sweetness of tomatoes. Bright, lemony, fresh and fragrant, it's enough to lift almost any dish.

What could be more redolent of summer than **fresh herbs**? My kitchen is filled with them, and the fragrance carried on a breezy day always evokes an Eastern Mediterranean summer's day. Parsley, mint, coriander and dill are the most commonly used herbs in Eastern Mediterranean cuisine. Buy them fresh or, better still, grow your own in pots on your windowsill and use them at every opportunity.

There is nothing quite as delicious and vibrant as parsley. There are two main varieties, curly and Italian flat-leaf. Personally, I prefer the flat-leaf, it being more fragrant and sweeter tasting than its cousin.

Fresh and fruity mint is found almost everywhere, and although there are more than a thousand different varieties, the best known are apple mint in herb salads, common garden spearmint with lamb, and of course peppermint to make a refreshing tea. Lemon balm is also of the mint family, and while more lemony than minty, it is equally refreshing.

Coriander is another native of the Eastern Mediterranean, and every part is edible: the leaves, the root and the seeds – whole, crushed or ground. If you grow your own coriander in a pot, make sure that you pick and use only the young leaves. Older leaves can have an unpleasant, almost soapy taste.

Coriander seeds are warm, mild and sweetly aromatic, almost citrusy, like orange peel. When ground they form an integral part of dukkah (a spice blend), but as they are very mild, you'll need to use a lot more than a pinch in a recipe to have any noticeable influence. Add to any chilli dish, or combine with cumin as part of a falafel recipe.

The roots of the coriander are full of flavour, so if you have a bunch with the roots still on, cut them off, then wash and purée them with the leaves to give an extra zing to whatever you're cooking. It is particularly good for making a pesto, a traditional tarator, or a simple coriander and onion whip

Dill, with its delicate feathery leaves, has a very distinctive look. The taste, reminiscent of aniseed, can be overpowering, so use sparingly. It is best used fresh, as it loses much of its flavour when dried, and should, as a general rule, be added near to the end of the cooking process. It works really well with vegetables like fennel and broad beans, and complements fish too, but don't go too mad with it.

Sumac Tuna and Bulgur Tartare with Wild Rocket and Fennel Salad

This is a light version of the traditional lamb kibbeh, which is a common street food all over the Eastern Mediterranean. There are hundreds of kibbeh recipes and almost every village has its own. Here I have substituted fresh tuna for the lamb. To serve the tartare you'll need a cutting ring.

FOR THE TARTARE

200ml   water

60g   fine bulgur wheat

300g   fresh tuna, finely chopped

1   red onion, finely chopped

¼   teaspoon cayenne pepper

½   teaspoon sumac

¼   teaspoon ground chilli

2   teaspoons small capers, well rinsed

FOR THE SALAD

150g   wild rocket

1   small fennel bulb, finely sliced

4   pink radishes, finely sliced

3   tablespoons olive oil

4   tablespoons lemon juice

TO SERVE

½   teaspoon sumac

3–4   tablespoons olive oil

TO MAKE THE TARTARE

Boil the water in a pan, then drop in the bulgur wheat and remove from the heat. Allow to stand for 8–10 minutes. Place the bulgur in a cloth and twist until squeezed dry, then put it in to a bowl. Mix in the tuna, red onion, cayenne pepper, sumac, chilli and capers. Season to taste.

TO MAKE THE SALAD

Toss the rocket, fennel and radishes with the olive oil and lemon juice, and season to taste.

TO SERVE

Place a cutting ring in the middle of a serving plate. Fill with the tuna and bulgur tartare, smooth the top and remove the ring. Top with a small handful of the wild rocket and fennel salad, sprinkle with sumac and drizzle with olive oil.

For 6 to share

Courgette and Dill Begindi

Hünkar Begindi means, depending on whom you ask, either 'the Queen' or 'the Sovereign' 'was pleased' or 'liked it'. This dish was a favourite in the Ottoman Court when made with aubergine and kashkaval, a mild, Cheddar-like cheese.

800g courgettes, cubed

15g butter

2 teaspoons cornflour

250–300ml milk

100g Gruyère cheese, grated

small bunch of fresh dill, finely chopped

TO SERVE

fresh crusty bread

Steam the courgettes for 5 minutes, until soft. Remove and mash roughly with a fork. Put to one side and allow to cool. In a small pan, over a medium heat, melt the butter. Stir in the cornflour until you have a smooth consistency. Slowly add the milk, whisking at the same time, until you have a thick, smooth, lump-free sauce. If you want a thicker sauce, add less milk. Now stir in the grated cheese and remove from the heat.

Combine the sauce with the mashed courgettes and sprinkle with the fresh dill. Serve hot, with fresh crusty bread.

For 8 to share

Sautéed King Prawns with Orange and Sumac Butter

This is as simple as it gets. The fresh, citrusy orange and sumac butter is the perfect partner to the delicate sweet king prawns. Try the butter with any grilled fish too.

FOR THE BUTTER

- 6 saffron threads
- ½ tablespoon ground sumac
- 50ml dry white wine
- zest and juice of ½ orange
- 100g butter, softened
- 4 garlic cloves, crushed
- 1 tablespoon fresh parsley leaves, finely chopped
- 1 teaspoon cumin seeds, finely ground

FOR THE PRAWNS

- 16 king prawns, shelled
- 1 tablespoon olive oil

TO MAKE THE BUTTER

Place the saffron and sumac in a small bowl with the dry white wine and leave to stand for a few minutes so that the saffron infuses. Now add the orange zest and juice. Combine this with the softened butter, garlic, parsley and cumin, and season.

Shape the butter into a sausage shape, wrap in clingfilm and chill in the fridge until firm.

TO COOK THE PRAWNS

In a heavy pan, sauté the prawns in a tablespoon of olive oil over a medium to high heat for 2–3 minutes, stirring all the time. Add about 75g of the chilled orange and sumac butter to the pan, turn off the heat and allow the butter to gently melt.

Transfer the king prawns to a warm serving plate and drizzle with the orange and sumac butter from the pan.

To serve, thinly slice the remaining chilled butter and place on the top of the prawns. For a main dish, this is delicious accompanied by a simple green salad and some Jerusalem Artichoke and Tahini Hummus (see p.171 for the recipe).

For 8 to share

Haloumi, Walnut and Frisee Lettuce Salad with Nigella Seed Vinaigrette

FOR THE VINAIGRETTE

1 tablespoon nigella seeds

1 tablespoon white wine vinegar

3 tablespoons olive oil

3 sprigs of fresh dill, finely chopped

1 garlic clove, crushed

FOR THE SALAD

1 large head of frisee lettuce, finely shredded lengthways

4 pears, quartered and finely sliced

100g white grapes, halved

150g shelled walnuts, lightly toasted

100g haloumi cheese, shaved as thin as you can manage

bunch of fresh chervil, leaves only

TO MAKE THE VINAIGRETTE

Whisk together all the ingredients, season and put to one side.

TO MAKE THE SALAD

In a large bowl, gently toss together the lettuce, pears, grapes and walnuts, and season to taste. Drizzle the vinaigrette over the salad and again gently toss to combine. Serve the salad in small bowls, garnished with the haloumi and chervil. The haloumi should be shaved so thin it's almost transparent.

For 8 to share

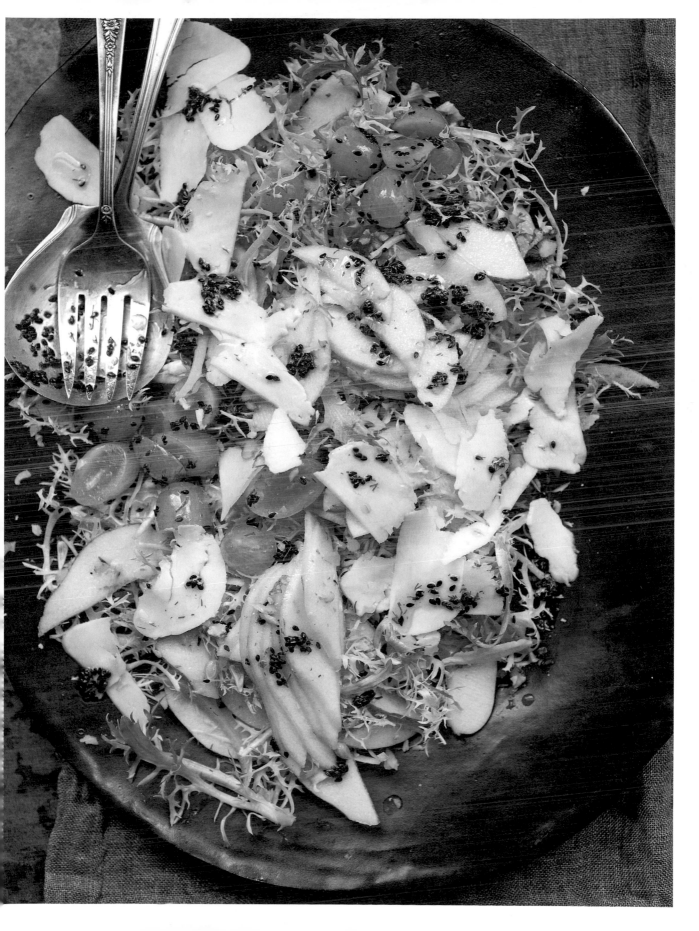

Caramelised Onion Salad with Sumac and Pomegranate Dressing

The combination of sumac and tomato was made in heaven. This salad is best in summer time when you can buy tomatoes that have not been grown in greenhouses, when they are sweet and delicious. I discovered this salad on my very first trip to Istanbul and I was blown away.

FOR THE SALAD

2 red onions, thinly sliced

2 tablespoons olive oil

½ teaspoon sugar

6 ripe plum tomatoes, cubed

FOR THE DRESSING

1 teaspoon ground sumac

½ teaspoon ground cumin

4 tablespoons olive oil

2 tablespoons pomegranate molasses (see p. 175 for the recipe)

Juice of ½ lemon

TO SERVE

½ pomegranate, seeds only

small bunch of fresh parsley, chopped

TO PREPARE THE SALAD

In a frying pan, sauté the onions in the olive oil on a medium heat for 10 minutes. Add the sugar and cook for a further 10 minutes, stirring from time to time until the onions are caramelised and soft. Remove from the heat and allow to cool completely.

Combine the tomatoes with the caramelised onions in a large bowl.

TO MAKE THE DRESSING

Combine all the ingredients and pour over the tomatoes and caramelised onion.

TO SERVE

Gently toss the salad and sprinkle with the pomegranate seeds and parsley.

For 6 to share

Chickpea, Sweet Potato and Spinach Cakes with Creamed Parsnip and Coriander Dip

FOR THE DIP

2 large parsnips, chopped

1 large garlic clove, crushed

juice of ½ lemon

3 tablespoons olive oil

small bunch of fresh coriander

¼ teaspoon coriander seeds

FOR THE CAKES

3 large sweet potatoes, cubed

400g tinned chickpeas, drained

300g fresh spinach leaves, cooked

6 tablespoons breadcrumbs

1 teaspoon ground cumin

1 teaspoon ground coriander

½ teaspoon ground cardamom

plain flour, for dusting

3–4 tablespoons olive oil

TO MAKE THE DIP

Cook the parsnips in boiling water for about 20 minutes, until soft. Drain, then purée in a food processor with the garlic, lemon juice and olive oil. Season to taste, then stir in the fresh coriander and coriander seeds.

TO MAKE THE CAKES

Cook the sweet potatoes in boiling water for about 20 minutes, until soft. Drain and roughly mash. Add the chickpeas, spinach, breadcrumbs and spices and combine well. Refrigerate for at least 30 minutes, then shape the mixture into 12 small patties and dust with the flour.

In a non-stick pan, heat the olive oil and pan fry the spinach and potato cakes on a medium/high heat for 2 minutes on each side, until golden.

Serve hot, with the parsnip and coriander dip.

For 6 to share

Seared Scallops with Hazelnut Dukkah on Sumac Onions

FOR THE DUKKAH

100g hazelnuts, blanched
1 tablespoon cumin seeds
2 tablespoons coriander seeds
2 tablespoons nigella seeds
1 tablespoon sesame seeds
2 tablespoons desiccated coconut
(note: here it is really good if you can use fresh coconut, grated, instead of the desiccated coconut)

FOR THE ONIONS

3 red onions, sliced
2 tablespoons olive oil
1 tablespoon pomegranate molasses (see p. 175 for the recipe)
1 teaspoon ground sumac

FOR THE SCALLOPS

12 large scallops
2 tablespoons olive oil

TO MAKE THE DUKKAH

In a dry, non-stick pan, toast the first five ingredients for 2 minutes on a medium/high heat, stirring constantly. Add the coconut in the last 40 seconds. Remove to a bowl and allow to cool completely.

Once cooled, place in a food processor, season, and blend to a coarse powder.

TO MAKE THE ONIONS

In a pan, on a medium heat, sauté the onions in the olive oil for 8–10 minutes, until soft. Add the pomegranate molasses and cook for a further 2 minutes, by which time the onions will have started to caramelise. Stir in the sumac and remove from the heat.

TO COOK THE SCALLOPS

Brush the scallops with olive oil and fry in a hot pan for about 2 minutes on each side, depending on size, until lightly golden.

Spoon some sumac onions on to a large platter, top with the scallops and sprinkle with the hazelnut dukkah.

For 8 to share

Coriander and Onion Whip

This dip is the perfect accompaniment to grilled seafood and fish, served simply with some fresh flatbread.

4 slices stale white bread, crusts removed

large bunch of fresh coriander, leaves only

1 red onion, chopped

1 free range egg yolk

100ml olive oil

TO SERVE

1 teaspoon ground sumac

Soak the bread in a bowl of cold water for 1 minute. Remove and squeeze dry. Place in a food processor along with the coriander and onion and blend until smooth. Add the egg yolk and pulse again. Drizzle in the olive oil, and season with salt and pepper.

TO SERVE

Place the coriander and onion whip in a serving bowl and sprinkle with the sumac.

For 8 to share

Smoked Haddock and Sumac Whip

350g smoked haddock, skin and bones removed

2 tablespoons olive oil

juice of 1 lemon

small bunch of fresh oregano, leaves only, finely chopped

150g thick yoghurt or suzme (strained yoghurt, see instructions on p.183)

TO SERVE

1 teaspoon sumac

fresh crusty bread

Place the fish in a small saucepan and just cover with water. Bring to the boil, then turn down the heat and simmer for 2–3 minutes. Drain and discard the water. Allow the fish to cool enough to handle, then flake into a bowl and allow to cool completely.

Combine the flaked haddock with the olive oil, lemon juice, oregano and yoghurt or suzme, and season to taste.

Spoon into a serving bowl, sprinkle with sumac and serve with some fresh crusty bread.

For 8 to share

Pistachio Dukkah-Crusted Duck with Sumac Onion Jam

FOR THE JAM

4 medium onions, thinly sliced

15g butter

2 teaspoons sugar

300ml sherry

30g dried cherries, chopped

1 teaspoon sumac

FOR THE DUKKAH

100g pistachios

1 tablespoon cumin seeds

2 tablespoons coriander seeds

2 tablespoons nigella seeds

1 tablespoon sesame seeds

2 tablespoons desiccated coconut

FOR THE DUCK

4 duck breasts, with skin

1 tablespoon olive oil

TO MAKE THE JAM

In a pan, sauté the onions in the butter on a medium heat for 8–10 minutes, stirring all the time. Add the sugar and continue cooking for a further 2 minutes. Now add the sherry and the cherries and reduce the heat to low. Cook for 45–50 minutes, or until the mixture becomes sticky and caramelised. Finally, stir in the sumac and season to taste. Put to one side to cool.

TO MAKE THE DUKKAH

In a dry, non-stick pan, toast all the dukkah ingredients for 2 minutes on a high heat, stirring constantly. Remove to a bowl and cool. Once cooled, place in a food processor, season and blend until you have a coarse powder.

TO COOK THE DUCK

Preheat the oven to 180°C fan/gas mark 6.

Rub all but 1 tablespoon of the dukkah powder over the duck breasts.

In a heavy, non-stick, ovenproof pan, sauté the duck in the olive oil on a high heat for 2–3 minutes on each side. Now, with the skin side up, sprinkle on the remaining dukkah and transfer the pan to the oven. Roast for 12 minutes, then remove and leave to rest for 5–6 minutes before serving.

TO SERVE

Slice the pistachio dukkah-crusted duck. Spoon some of the sumac onion jam on to the middle of a serving plate and arrange the warm sliced duck on top.

For 8 to share

Wild Greens and Feta Börek

For this recipe you can use spinach or any seasonal wild greens that are available.

200g fresh wild watercress

300g fresh wild rocket

  2 tablespoons olive oil

200g feta cheese, crumbled

  ½ teaspoon black pepper, crushed

  ½ teaspoon red pepper, crushed

  2 eggs

250ml milk

  6 tablespoons melted unsalted butter

  20 sheets of filo pastry

  2 tablespoons nigella seeds

Preheat the oven to 200°C fan/gas mark 7.

In a pan, sauté the watercress and rocket in the olive oil for 2 minutes on a medium heat, until just wilted. Once cool enough to handle, squeeze out the excess liquid. Place in a large bowl and combine with the feta cheese and the black and red pepper.

In a separate bowl beat the eggs, then stir in the milk and melted butter.

Lightly oil a 25 × 35cm baking tray and lay in the first sheet of filo pastry. Brush generously with the egg mixture and top with another sheet. Repeat this until you have used 10 of the filo sheets.

Spoon on the wild greens and feta mixture and top with the remaining 10 filo sheets, brushing with the egg mixture between each sheet, as before. Pour any remaining egg mixture over the final layer and sprinkle with the nigella seeds.

Bake in the oven for 30–35 minutes, until golden brown. Remove and allow to cool before cutting into squares.

For 8 to share

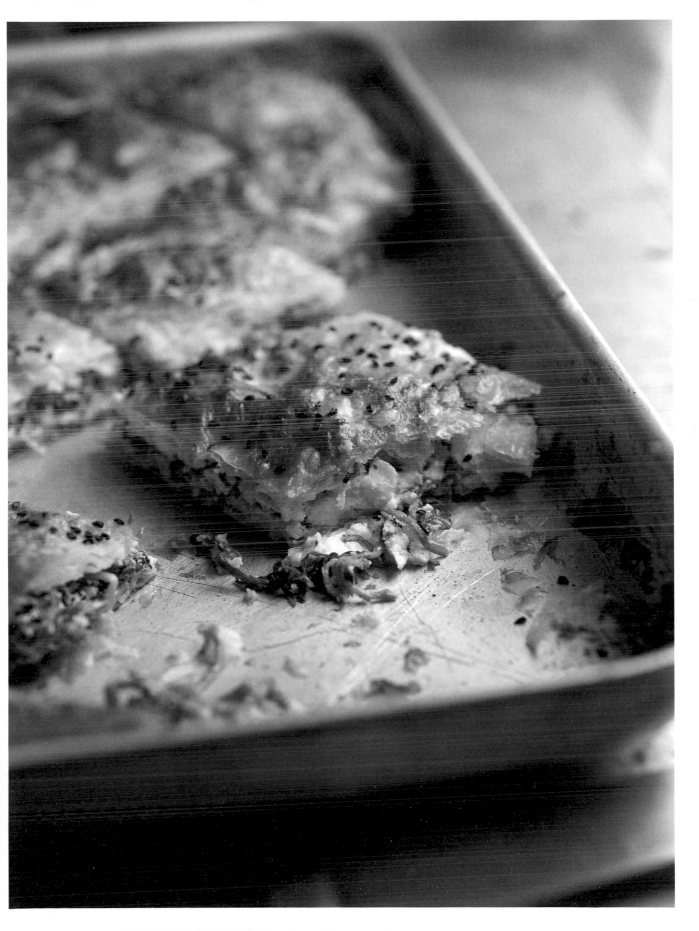

Anchovy and Parsley-Stuffed Veal Meatballs with Olive Oil and Garlic Cream

FOR THE CREAM

2 egg yolks

150ml olive oil

juice of 1 lemon

1 garlic clove, crushed

FOR THE MEATBALLS

500g ground veal

1 egg

small bunch of fresh parsley, finely chopped

100g Gruyère cheese, finely grated

2 hard-boiled eggs, finely chopped

3 anchovies, finely chopped

1 teaspoon ground cumin

3 tablespoons plain flour, for dusting

4–5 tablespoons olive oil

TO MAKE THE CREAM

Place the egg yolks in a food processor and, with the motor on low, slowly drizzle in the olive oil until you have a smooth consistency. Stir in the lemon juice and garlic, and season to taste. Transfer to a bowl and chill until needed.

TO PREPARE THE MEATBALLS

In a large bowl, combine the veal, raw egg, fresh parsley and cheese. In a separate bowl, combine the hard-boiled eggs, anchovies and cumin. Season and mix well.

TO ASSEMBLE THE MEATBALLS

Take a tablespoon of the veal mixture and shape it into a ball. Then, with a finger, make an indentation in the centre and fill with the egg and anchovy mix. Close up the meatball, ensuring the stuffing is fully enclosed, and roll it around in your hands before rolling in the flour. Repeat until the ingredients are used up.

In a non-stick pan, heat the olive oil and cook the meatballs, a few at a time, for 10 minutes on a medium heat, until browned and evenly cooked.

Serve the meatballs hot, with the chilled olive oil and garlic cream, and Crispy Herb-Coated Courgettes with Coriander and Lemon Confit Dressing (p.101), pictured pages 80–1.

For 8 to share

Fresh Crab and Coriander Gözleme

300g fresh white crabmeat, cooked

small bunch of fresh coriander, leaves only, chopped

1 dessert apple, grated

juice of ½ lemon

2 large circular sheets of yufka or filo pastry

4–5 tablespoons melted clarified butter or ghee

Combine the cooked crabmeat, coriander, grated apple and lemon juice in a bowl and season to taste.

Lay 2 circular sheets of yufka on top of each other and cut in half. Lay the halves on top of each other and cut into 3 equal wedges, so that you end up with 12 in total. Now cut off the rounded edges at the top of each wedge so that you make triangles.

Working with one pastry triangle at a time, spoon some of the crab mixture into the middle and brush the edges with melted butter. Fold the points of the triangle so that they overlap and enclose the filling. Brush the tops with melted butter and arrange on a platter. Repeat until you have 12 filled pastries.

In a non-stick pan, sauté the gözleme in the remaining butter on a medium heat for 2–3 minutes on each side, until golden and crispy. Serve hot or cold.

Makes 12

Gruyère and Mixed Herb Kadaifi Pies

150g Gruyère cheese, grated

100g feta cheese, crumbled

½ small bunch of fresh
     oregano, leaves and flowers
     only, finely chopped

½ small bunch of fresh chives,
     finely chopped

½ small bunch of fresh mint,
     finely chopped

150g melted unsalted butter

400g kadaifi pastry

4 eggs

300ml milk

1 tablespoon za'atar

TO SERVE

4–5 tablespoons runny honey

Preheat the oven to 180°C fan/gas mark 6.

Combine the Gruyère, feta and fresh herbs in a bowl.

Brush 6 flat tart dishes, approximately 12cm in diameter, generously with the melted butter. Take half of the kadaifi pastry and firmly push a layer of strands into the bottom of each dish, applying some pressure with the back of a spoon. Spoon the cheese and herb mixture evenly between the 6 dishes. Cover with the remaining kadaifi, again pressing the pastry down well. Generously brush each pie with melted butter. Keep pressing down to hold the unruly kadaifi pastry in place – you have to be quite forceful with the kadaifi. You may find that you don't need all the butter.

Beat the eggs together with the milk and za'atar, and season. Pour this on to each pie so that it soaks in.

Bake the pies for about 20 minutes, until they are golden and crispy.

Optional: drizzle with a little honey and serve hot. (No, you didn't misread it, honey – give it a try!)

Makes 6

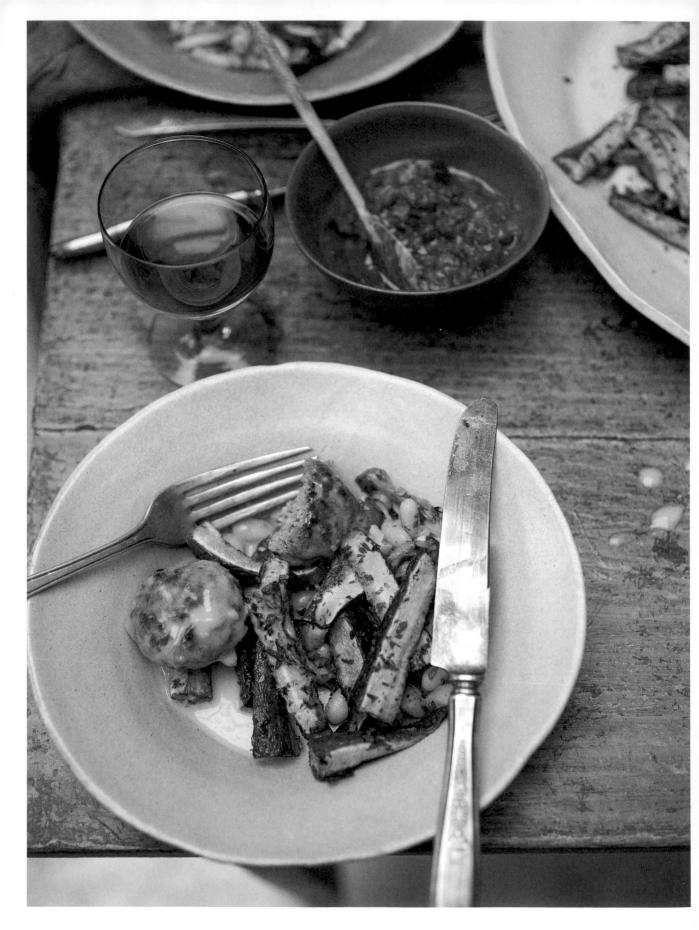

Crispy Herb-Coated Courgettes with Coriander and Lemon Confit Dressing

FOR THE LEMON CONFIT

150ml water

80g sugar

1 lemon, finely sliced

FOR THE DRESSING

3 lemon confit slices (see above)

4 tablespoons olive oil

1 ripe tomato, skinned and finely chopped

small bunch of fresh coriander, finely chopped

FOR THE COURGETTES

3 medium courgettes

1 large egg

3 tablespoons panko breadcrumbs (or homemade breadcrumbs)

small bunch of fresh thyme, leaves only, finely chopped

small bunch of fresh parsley, finely chopped

vegetable oil, for deep-frying

TO MAKE THE CONFIT

In a small saucepan, slowly bring to the boil the water and sugar, stirring well to dissolve the sugar. Reduce to a simmer and continue to stir for about 3 minutes, until you have a thick syrup. Add the lemon slices and cook on a low heat for 10 minutes, until they are translucent. Drain the lemon slices and discard the syrup. The lemon confit slices you don't use in this recipe will keep for a week.

TO MAKE THE DRESSING

Finely chop 3 of the lemon confit slices and place them in a bowl with the olive oil, tomato and coriander. Mix well and season to taste.

TO PREPARE THE COURGETTES

Slice the courgettes into 3–4cm chunky strips. In a bowl, beat the egg and add the courgette. In a separate bowl, combine the panko breadcrumbs with the fresh herbs. Drop the egg-coated courgettes into the breadcrumbs and herbs and coat well.

Heat the vegetable oil in a deep-fat fryer to 180°C. Carefully drop a few courgette discs into the oil and cook for 2–3 minutes, until golden. Remove with a slotted wooden spoon and drain on kitchen paper. Repeat until all the courgette discs are cooked.

Serve the crispy courgettes hot, with the lemon confit dressing on the side to dip.

For 8 to share

Sumac Octopus with Pomegranate

Octopus can be very tough, so it is best poached before using it in a dish.
Use fresh octopus if possible; if using frozen, be sure to defrost thoroughly.

1 litre water

3 tablespoons white wine vinegar

juice of ½ lemon

2 bay leaves

3 black peppercorns

½ tablespoon sea salt

1 whole octopus, approx. 1.5kg

4 tablespoons white wine vinegar

2 tablespoons pomegranate molasses (see p.175 for the recipe)

1 tablespoon caster sugar

½ tablespoon ground sumac

1 red onion, finely sliced

TO SERVE

3–4 tablespoons olive oil

1 pomegranate, seeds only

small bunch of fresh oregano, leaves only, finely chopped

ground sumac (extra)

fresh bread

TO POACH THE OCTOPUS

Boil 1 litre of water in a saucepan and add the white wine vinegar, lemon juice, bay leaves, black peppercorns and sea salt. Reduce the heat and simmer for 10 minutes. Using tongs and holding the octopus by the head, dip it in the simmering poaching liquid 3 times, for about 15 seconds each time. This is known as scaring and will prevent the octopus tentacles curling up.

Next, place the octopus in the simmering water and allow to cook for 30–40 minutes. Drain and cool then remove the head and use just the body and tentacles. This method of cooking the octopus is the same whether you are going to grill it afterwards or just marinate it as here.

In a bowl, combine the white wine vinegar, pomegranate molasses, sugar and sumac. Stir until the sugar is completely dissolved. Season, then add the red onion and chill in the fridge for 30 minutes.

TO SERVE

Slice the octopus very thinly, almost sashimi style, and arrange on a platter. Pour over the pomegranate mixture, then drizzle with the olive oil. Scatter over the pomegranate seeds and oregano leaves. Season to taste and finally sprinkle with the extra sumac. Serve with fresh bread.

For 8 to share

Lentil and Parsley Tabbouleh with Wild Garlic and Sesame Suzme

FOR THE TABBOULEH

50g Puy lentils

bunch of fresh parsley, leaves only, finely chopped

1 large ripe tomato, skinned and finely chopped

2 shallots, finely chopped

juice of 1 lemon

2 tablespoons olive oil

1 teaspoon sumac

FOR THE SUZME

10g butter

200g wild garlic, leaves only (substitute with spinach if you can't get wild garlic)

400g thick yoghurt or suzme (strained yoghurt, see instructions on p.183)

1 tablespoon black sesame seeds

TO PREPARE THE TABBOULEH

Bring a large saucepan of water to the boil and cook the lentils according to the packet instructions, for around 20 minutes, until soft. Drain, put into a bowl and allow to cool. Once the lentils have cooled, combine with the parsley, tomato, shallots, lemon juice, olive oil and sumac.

TO MAKE THE SUZME

In a large saucepan, melt the butter and sauté the wild garlic leaves for 2–3 minutes, until just wilted. Season to taste and leave to cool completely. Once cooled, mix with the suzme and the sesame seeds.

Serve the lentil tabbouleh accompanied by the wild garlic and sesame suzme.

For 8 to share

Skordalia Cavolo Nero Cakes topped with Shredded Duck Confit and Pomegranate

Cavolo nero is a strong-flavoured Italian cabbage with dark green leaves. Confit is any meat slowly cooked in fat and it really is worth using. Duck confit can be bought in tins, or you can make it yourself. Alternatively, use conventionally roasted duck legs.

FOR THE CAKES

- 2 large baking potatoes
- 200g cavolo nero, chopped into small pieces
- bunch of fresh basil, chopped
- 2 garlic cloves, crushed
- 5 tablespoons ground almonds
- 6 tablespoons olive oil
- 1 tablespoon lemon juice
- 4–5 tablespoons panko breadcrumbs
- 2 tablespoons olive oil (extra)

FOR THE DUCK

- 4 duck confit quarters
- 2 teaspoons pomegranate molasses (see p. 175 for the recipe)
- 1 pomegranate, seeds only

TO COOK THE CAKES

Preheat the oven to 180°C fan/gas mark 6.

Bake the potatoes in the oven for at least an hour, until the insides are soft. Let them cool, then scoop out the insides, discarding the skins. Mash the potato into a smooth purée, and season to taste.

Place the cavolo nero in a small saucepan, cover with water and bring to the boil. Reduce to a simmer and cook for 3 minutes, until soft. Drain and stir into the mashed potatoes along with the basil, garlic, ground almonds, olive oil and lemon juice. Combine well, or if preferred blend in a food processor to a smooth purée, and season to taste. Shape into golfball-sized cakes and flatten slightly

Coat the cakes in the panko breadcrumbs and lightly fry them, a few at a time, in the extra olive oil on a medium heat for 2–3 minutes, until golden brown. Remove and arrange on a platter.

TO PREPARE THE DUCK

Shred the duck confit into small pieces with your fingers, discarding the skin and bones, and place in a bowl. Add the molasses and pomegranate seeds, stir to coat well and season to taste.

Serve the skordalia cakes hot or cold, with the duck generously piled on top.

For 8 to share

Sumac and Pistachio Dukkah
Prawns with Tahini Sauce

FOR THE DUKKAH

4 tablespoons black sesame
  seeds

3 tablespoons cumin seeds

3 tablespoons pistachios

1 teaspoon sea salt

1 teaspoon ground sumac

FOR THE SAUCE

50ml tahini

1 garlic clove, crushed

½ tablespoon ground cumin

3 tablespoons olive oil

juice of 1 lemon

100ml cold water

FOR THE PRAWNS

1 tablespoon olive oil

16 king prawns, peeled and
  de-veined

TO SERVE

nasturtium flowers

fresh flatbread

TO MAKE THE DUKKAH

In a dry frying pan, toast the sesame seeds, cumin seeds and pistachios on a high heat for 1 minute. Remove and allow to cool before roughly grinding them with the sea salt and sumac.

TO MAKE THE SAUCE

Combine all the ingredients, adding the lemon juice last and season to taste. The consistency should be like single cream, so add a little more cold water to further thin it if required.

TO COOK THE PRAWNS

In a non stick pan, heat the olive oil and cook the prawns for 3–4 minutes on a medium heat, until lightly golden. Remove from the pan using a slotted wooden spoon and arrange on a platter. Drizzle with the tahini sauce, sprinkle with the dukkah then scatter the nasturtium flowers around.

A simple yet stunning sharing dish best accompanied simply with some fresh flatbread.

For 8 to share

Crushed Broad Beans and Avocado with Parmesan and Sumac Biscuits

FOR THE BISCUITS

125g Parmesan, grated

125g butter, cubed

125g plain flour (and extra for dusting)

½ tablespoon ground sumac

5–6 tablespoons melted butter, for brushing

1 tablespoon black sesame seeds

FOR THE BEANS

1kg fresh or frozen broad beans, shelled

1 ripe avocado

juice of 1 small lemon

2 tablespoons olive oil

1 tablespoon tahini

½ teaspoon ground sumac

TO MAKE THE BISCUITS

Preheat the oven to 180°C fan/gas mark 6.

Place the Parmesan, butter, flour and sumac in a food processor and blend until well combined. Tip on to a flour-dusted surface and work into a smooth dough. Separate into 4 equal pieces, roll each to about ½cm thickness between parchment paper, lift the top parchment off then brush with a little melted butter and sprinkle with sesame seeds.

Arrange the dough on a baking tray and cook for 8 minutes, until just golden. Remove and cool slightly before breaking each piece into 4–5 smaller biscuits.

TO PREPARE THE BEANS

Heat a large saucepan of water, add the broad beans and boil for 10 minutes. Immediately drain and rinse under cold water. Peel the skins off the beans and discard.

In a food processor, briefly blend the beans with the avocado, lemon juice, olive oil, tahini and sumac, so that the beans are still a little chunky.

Season to taste and serve with the Parmesan and sumac biscuits.

For 8 to share

Sumac-Crusted Tuna
with Pink Grapefruit Salsa

FOR THE SALSA

2 pink grapefruits, peeled and finely chopped

2 blood oranges, peeled and finely chopped

small bunch of fresh parsley, finely chopped

1 red onion, finely sliced

juice of 1 small lemon

1 teaspoon ground sumac

FOR THE TUNA

2 tablespoons ground sumac

1 teaspoon ground cumin

½ teaspoon ground black pepper

400g tuna steaks, cut into long strips

2 tablespoons olive oil

TO MAKE THE SALSA

Combine the grapefruit, orange, parsley and red onion in a bowl. Toss with the lemon juice, add the crushed sumac and season to taste. Set aside.

TO COOK THE TUNA

Preheat the grill to high.

In a separate bowl, mix the sumac, cumin and black pepper. Brush the strips of tuna with the olive oil, then coat with the spice mix. Grill the tuna on high for 2–3 minutes on each side.

Serve hot, with the grapefruit salsa.

For 8 to share

Cardamom Duck with Orange and Sumac Infused Sauce

This is so easy to prepare and a real crowd-pleaser. Serve with a rice pilaf.

4 large duck breasts, with skin

FOR THE SAUCE

4 shallots, finely chopped

¼ teaspoon cardamom seeds, lightly crushed

200ml chicken stock

juice of 1 large orange

1 teaspoon ground sumac

20g butter

TO COOK THE DUCK

Score the skin of the duck breasts and season with salt and pepper. Heat a heavy pan over a low to medium heat and sear the duck breasts on both sides for 10 minutes, until browned. Increase the heat to high and cook skin side down for 2 more minutes, until the skin is crisp. Remove the duck from the pan and set aside to rest in a warm place. Leave any juices and fat in the pan.

TO MAKE THE SAUCE

Keep the high heat under the pan in which you cooked the duck and sauté the shallots for 5 minutes. Add the cardamom seeds and stir for a minute longer. Skim off the excess fat and add the stock and orange juice. Season to taste and simmer for 8–10 minutes, until the liquid has reduced by half. Add the sumac, stir to combine and remove from the heat.

Strain the sauce through a sieve and discard any solids. Finally, whisk in the butter.

Slice the duck and pour over the sauce. Serve with Lentil, Orzo and Pinenut Pilaf with Saffron Onions (see p.32)

For 8 to share

Potato Gnocchi with Coconut and Mascarpone Sauce and Coriander Coconut Dukkah

For this, use fresh coconut for the best flavour although desiccated coconut can be substituted if more convenient.

FOR THE GNOCCHI

- 500g starchy potatoes, such as russets
- 1 egg yolk
- pinch of salt
- 150g plain flour

FOR THE SAUCE

- 4 tablespoons coconut milk
- 150g mascarpone cheese
- 40g fresh coconut, grated
- ½ small bunch of fresh coriander, finely chopped

FOR THE DUKKAH

- 100g blanched almonds
- 2 tablespoons coriander seeds
- 2 tablespoons cumin seeds
- 2 tablespoons grated fresh coconut
- 2 tablespoons sesame seeds
- ½ teaspoon salt
- ½ teaspoon black pepper

TO SERVE

- nasturtium flowers, to serve

TO MAKE THE GNOCCHI

Preheat the oven to 200°C fan/gas mark 7. Bake the potatoes for 1½ hours. Remove from the oven and leave until cool enough to handle. Halve the potatoes, and scoop out the flesh into a bowl. Put the potato flesh through a potato ricer, to mash finely. Add the egg yolk, salt and three-quarters of the flour, mixing well to form a smooth dough, adding the remaining flour if required.

Divide the dough into 4 pieces, then roll into sausage shapes, about 2½cm thick. Cut the sausages into 1cm long pieces and arrange on a floured tray. Gently press each of the gnocchi with a fork to flatten slightly.

Boil a saucepan of water and drop in the gnocchi. Cook for 2–3 minutes, until they rise to the surface of the water, then drain immediately.

TO MAKE THE SAUCE

In a small pan, cook the coconut milk and mascarpone on a medium heat for 3–4 minutes. Season to taste and stir in the grated coconut and coriander.

TO MAKE THE DUKKAH

Place all the ingredients in a hot dry frying pan and gently toast for 2 minutes, stirring all the time. Cool and grind roughly with a mortar and pestle.

Add the cooked gnocchi to the coconut and mascarpone sauce and coat well. Serve sprinkled with the coriander coconut dukkah, and decorate with a few nasturtium petals.

For 8 to share

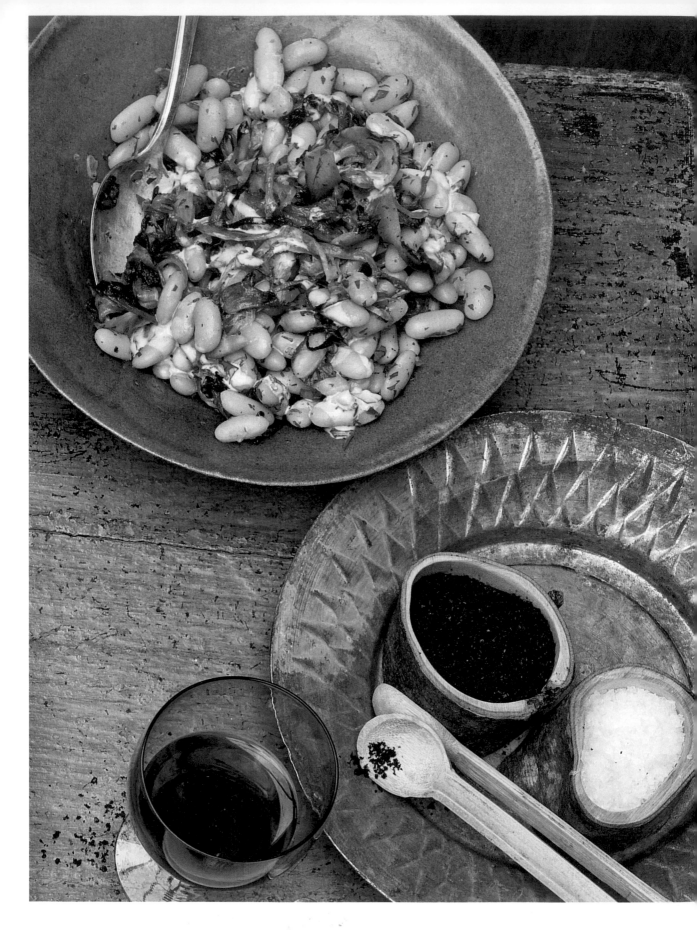

White Bean, Parsley and Caramelised Fennel Salad with Lemon and Tahini Dressing

This is my version of a piyaz, a name that is generally given to all bean salads. In Persian the word means onion, which is also a common ingredient. Piyaz can be either eaten as a main course or as a salad to accompany kofte. I have used dried beans in this recipe but you can use canned beans to speed things up.

FOR THE SALAD

- 3 tablespoons olive oil
- 1 medium fennel bulb, thinly sliced
- 1 onion, thinly sliced
- 10g butter
- zest and juice of 1 small lemon
- 350g white haricot beans, soaked overnight
- small bunch of fresh parsley, finely chopped
- ½ teaspoon sumac

FOR THE DRESSING

- 2 tablespoons tahini
- zest and juice of 1 small lemon
- ½ garlic clove
- 1 tablespoon olive oil
- ⅓ cup water

TO PREPARE THE SALAD

Heat the oil in a saucepan and sauté the fennel and onion over a low heat for 10–15 minutes, stirring from time to time, until the fennel and onions are soft and caramelised. Season to taste and remove from the heat before stirring in the butter, lemon zest and lemon juice. Put to one side to cool.

Drain the soaked beans and place in a large saucepan. Cover with cold water and bring to the boil. Reduce to a simmer and cook for 25–30 minutes, until the beans are soft. Drain, then put the beans into a large serving bowl. Allow to cool, then add the caramelised fennel and onion, parsley and sumac. Combine well and season to taste.

TO MAKE THE DRESSING

Combine all the dressing ingredients in a separate bowl, adding more water if needed to get a thinner dressing consistency, then drizzle over the salad and serve.

For 8 to share

Veal and Pistachio Mini Burgers
with Fried Sumac Onions

2 teaspoons olive oil

1 large onion, thinly sliced

1 teaspoon ground sumac

FOR THE BURGERS

950g veal, finely chopped

2 large eggs

5cm fresh ginger, peeled and finely grated

2 green chillies, de-seeded and finely chopped

1 teaspoon ground cumin

1 onion, grated

120g pistachio nuts, skinless, chopped

TO SERVE

4 Turkish pitta bread or 1 large focaccia flat loaf

20 sprigs parsley

tahini mayonnaise
(see p.179 for the recipe)

TO COOK THE ONIONS

Heat the olive oil in a frying pan over a low to medium heat, then add the sliced onion and sauté until golden. Sprinkle with the sumac and remove from the heat.

TO MAKE THE BURGERS

Preheat the grill to medium/high.

Mix the veal in a bowl with the eggs, ginger, chillies, cumin, onion and pistachios. Knead to combine really well, then shape the mixture into 16 small burgers.

Grill the burgers for at least 3 minutes on each side, until golden and cooked right through.

TO SERVE

Make the burger rolls by cutting burger shapes from pitta bread or the flat focaccia bread, using a small, round pastry cutter. Top half a toasted burger bun with a veal and pistachio burger and a helping of fried sumac onions, adding a sprig of flat parsley and a spoonful of Tahini Mayonnaise. Cover with the remaining half bun and serve.

Makes 16

Broad Bean, Wild Garlic and Fennel Dip

Broad beans are a much-loved ingredient in Eastern Mediterranean cuisine.
This recipe is based on a classic Turkish dip, and is best made with fresh beans
for a creamier consistency. Either way, always remove the hard outer skins
of the broad beans once they are cooked. If you can't find fresh broad beans
then use frozen.

300g *fresh broad beans, shelled (approx. 1kg unshelled)*

2 *tablespoons olive oil*

1 *medium fennel bulb, finely sliced*

2 *shallots, finely sliced*

½ *teaspoon brown sugar*

300g *wild garlic leaves*

50g *pack of fresh dill, finely chopped*

TO SERVE

fresh bread

Bring a small saucepan of water to boil and drop in the broad beans. Cook for 4–5 minutes, until soft. Drain the beans and allow to cool. Reserve half a cup of the water that the beans were cooked in.

When the beans are cool enough to handle, remove and discard the outer skins.

Heat the olive oil in a deep frying pan, and over a low heat cook the fennel and shallots with the sugar sprinkled on top for 10 minutes, stirring from time to time. Next, add the wild garlic leaves and cook for a further 5 minutes. Season to taste and remove from the heat. If wild garlic is out of season, use wild rocket, which will give a light, peppery taste.

Place the cooked broad beans in a food processor with the cooked fennel, shallots and wild garlic and blend to a smooth purée. Add the reserved water as required, until you achieve the consistency of double cream.

Sprinkle with the fresh dill and serve with fresh bread.

For 8–10 to share

Sumac Scallops with Walnut and Roasted Garlic Sauce

This is particularly delicious served with chilli cress, but if you can't get any, ordinary cress will do.

FOR THE SAUCE

1 garlic bulb

200g walnuts, finely ground

3 tablespoons olive oil

zest and juice of 1 small lemon

200ml chicken stock

FOR THE SCALLOPS

16 medium-sized scallops

2 tablespoons olive oil

1 teaspoon ground sumac

TO SERVE

2 pots of chilli cress

50g walnut pieces, toasted

TO MAKE THE SAUCE

Preheat the oven to 180°C fan/gas mark 6.

Place the whole garlic bulb on a small baking tray and roast in the oven for 20 minutes. Remove, and when cool enough to handle, squeeze the roasted garlic flesh out of the bulb, discarding the skin.

In a small saucepan, mix together the garlic, walnuts, olive oil, lemon zest and juice, until you have a smooth creamy mixture. On a medium heat, stirring all the time, add the chicken stock. Cook for 5 minutes and season to taste.

TO COOK THE SCALLOPS

Brush the scallops with olive oil. Heat a non-stick frying pan over a medium heat and cook the scallops for 2 minutes on each side. Remove from the heat and sprinkle with sumac.

TO SERVE

Arrange the hot scallops on a platter. Drizzle with the walnut and garlic sauce, and scatter with some chilli cress and toasted walnuts.

For 8 to share

Sumac Crab and Avocado
with Tahini Dressing

1 egg

150ml olive oil

juice of 1 lemon

100g fresh brown crabmeat,
cooked

1 tablespoon tahini

FOR THE CRAB

450g fresh white crabmeat,
cooked

juice of ½ lemon

1 teaspoon ground sumac

50g pack of fresh basil, leaves
only, finely chopped

50g pack of fresh parsley, leaves
only, finely chopped

2 large avocados

extra lemon juice for the
avocados

TO SERVE

black sesame crisp flatbread
(see p. 169 for the recipe)

2 lemons, cut into quarters

TO MAKE THE DRESSING

Whisk the egg, drizzling in the olive oil at the same time, until you have
a thick consistency. Add the lemon juice and the cooked brown crabmeat.
Combine and season well before finally stirring in the tahini.

TO PREPARE THE CRAB

Combine the cooked white crabmeat, lemon juice, sumac and herbs, and
season to taste. Peel and thinly slice the avocados, squeezing lemon juice
over the top to prevent discoloration, if not using immediately.

TO SERVE

Top pieces of Black Sesame Crisp Flatbread with some of the sumac crab and
the avocado slices, and drizzle with the tahini dressing. Serve with lemon
quarters.

For 8 to share

Lemon Balm Sorbet, Black Sesame Macaroon Crumble and Lemon Balm Oil

FOR THE SORBET

600ml water

160ml light corn syrup

small bunch of lemon balm, leaves only

110g caster sugar

juice of 2 lemons

FOR THE CRUMBLE

50g ground black sesame seeds

80g ground almonds

220g icing sugar

3 medium egg whites

2 tablespoons caster sugar

FOR THE OIL

1 bunch lemon balm

100ml rapeseed oil

TO SERVE

12–16 small lemon balm leaves

1 DAY IN ADVANCE

Blend the water and syrup together in a food processor or a blender. Pour into a saucepan and heat gently. Remove from the heat just before it boils. Add the lemon balm leaves, sugar and lemon juice. Stir until the sugar dissolves and allow to cool. You can leave the balm leaves in or discard as you choose.

Using an ice cream machine, churn the mixture as per your machine's instructions, for about 40–45 minutes. If you haven't got an ice cream machine, place the mixture in a plastic container, cover and place in the freezer. You'll need to stir the sorbet every half an hour until it's set.

TO MAKE THE CRUMBLE

Preheat the oven to 150°C fan/gas mark 3½.

Blend the sesame seeds, ground almonds and icing sugar in a food processor. Whisk the egg whites to hard peaks, add the caster sugar and continue whisking until glossy. Fold the sesame mixture into the egg whites a little at a time.

Line and lightly grease a 20 x 27cm baking tray. Spread the macaroon mixture over the tray – it should be about 2cm thick. Bake in the oven for 45 minutes. Remove and cool. Break into crumbled pieces and put to one side until needed.

TO MAKE THE OIL

Place the lemon balm into a food processor and blend until finely chopped. Add the rapeseed oil and pulse briefly to combine. Pour the mixture through a sieve and discard the solids, reserving only the scented oil.

TO SERVE

Arrange a few pieces of the macaroon crumble on each plate. Spoon on some lemon balm sorbet, drizzle with a touch of lemon balm oil, then scatter more of the crumble on top. Garnish with lemon balm leaves and serve.

For 8 to share

Sweet Eucalyptus & Liquid Gold

CARDAMOM AND HONEY

The great thing about **cardamom** is that it can be used in savoury and sweet dishes. For me it is both sweet and reminiscent of eucalyptus. Available in green and black varieties; ground, in whole pods or just the seeds. A member of the ginger family, it is highly perfumed, so you need to be careful how much you use. As part of a marinade, added to goat's cheese with a hint of maple syrup, sprinkled on baked figs, combined in a white chocolate mousse or simply added to your freshly ground coffee, it makes a dish exquisite.

There are almost as many types of **honey** as there are flowers. Mono floral honeys are more distinctive, for example heather, acacia, lavender and orange blossom. Try a few out until you find one that you really like, or of course you can stick to the more commonly sold poly floral honey which is derived from a variety of flowers.

It might sound self-evident, but honey has a delicate natural sweetness, completely different from manufactured sugars, that lends itself to all things culinary. It's incredibly versatile: drizzled on simple böreks, stirred into yoghurt, or, for a sensational display of flavours, try the lemon thyme infused burrata with honey, berries and balsamic vinegar.

Honey Mashed Broad Beans with Capers and Spring Onions

This recipe needs at least 6 hours in the fridge to set, so make sure you prepare it well in advance. This is one of the most common Turkish mezze in any high street eaterie.

250g dried broad beans, soaked overnight

3 shallots, finely chopped

2 garlic cloves, crushed

7 tablespoons olive oil

1 bay leaf

½ teaspoon turmeric

1 litre water

4 spring onions, finely sliced

2 tablespoons small capers, drained

zest and juice of ½ lemon

1 teaspoon runny honey

8–10 sprigs of fresh dill, finely chopped

TO SERVE

1 tablespoon capers, chopped, or use baby capers if you can

6–8 parsley sprigs, chopped

2 tablespoons olive oil

½ teaspoon nigella seeds

To ensure a smooth and silky purée, remove the skins from the pre-soaked broad beans. If they're not loose enough, boil for 10 minutes, drain and cool before removing them.

In a large pan, sauté the shallots and garlic for 2 minutes in 4 tablespoons of the olive oil over a medium heat. Add the bay leaf, turmeric and shelled broad beans. Season to taste, then cover with 1 litre of water. Simmer for about 1 hour, or until the beans are soft and the cooking liquid has mostly evaporated. Remove and discard the bay leaf.

In a small frying pan, sauté the spring onions and capers for 2–3 minutes in 2 tablespoons of olive oil on a medium heat. Transfer to a food processor along with the cooked beans and blend until smooth. Check the seasoning, then add the lemon zest, lemon juice and honey.

Using the remaining olive oil, brush a shallow rectangular tray approx. 20 × 30cm then line with cling film, sides and base, brush them with oil and scatter with the chopped dill. Pour in the bean purée, smooth over the top, cover with clingfilm and place in the fridge for at least 6 hours to set.

TO SERVE

Meanwhile, place in a bowl the nigella seeds, capers, parsley and oil, and mix. When ready to serve, cut out small round shapes with a pastry cutter. Turn the rounds over so that the dill is on top. Serve cold, sprinkled with the capers and seeds mixture.

For 6 to share

Raki and Honey Cured Salmon

This recipe is very simple, but you'll need to plan it 2 days in advance.
If you can't find raki, vodka can be used as a substitute.

25g light brown sugar

50g sea salt

¼ tablespoon dill seeds

½ small bunch of fresh dill, finely chopped

½ small bunch of fresh oregano, finely chopped

5–6 fresh oregano flowers, finely chopped

500–600g fillet of salmon

1 teaspoon runny honey

3 tablespoons raki

TO SERVE

Amaranth cress leaves or any cress leaves

fresh herb salad

2 DAYS IN ADVANCE

In a bowl, combine the sugar, salt, dill seeds, fresh dill, fresh oregano and oregano flowers. Having made sure that there are no bones remaining in the fish, lay the fillet skin side down on a large piece of clingfilm. Press the dill and oregano mixture into the fish, drizzle with the honey and spoon over the raki. Enclose the fish in the clingfilm in such a way as not to let the curing mixture escape. Place the fillet on a board, then cover with a second, weighted down with some tins. Refrigerate for 36 hours, turning every 12 hours.

After 36 hours remove the fish from the clingfilm, scrape off and discard the curing ingredients if you wish – I like to leave it for a crunchy effect – and pat dry with kitchen paper. Re-wrap the fish in clingfilm and put back in to the fridge, unweighted, for a further 12 hours.

After a total of 48 hours' curing, finely slice the salmon and serve with amaranth cress leaves and a fresh herb salad.

For 8 to share

Pistachio and Cardamom Lamb Manti

Manti are filled pasta dumplings and are extremely popular in Turkey. The dough is usually made using just plain flour, but this version, shown to me at the Çiragan Palace, also uses pistachios and gives the dumplings a wonderful taste and intriguing bright green colour. Served hot, topped with yoghurt and a drizzle of paprika oil, these are fabulous. This recipe does take some time to make, but it is well worth it. I like to make double quantities and freeze some. You will need a pasta machine, although a rolling pin can also be used.

FOR THE DOUGH

400g strong flour, plus extra for dusting

1 teaspoon sea salt

¼ teaspoon cardamom seeds, finely ground

60g pistachios, finely ground

4 eggs, lightly beaten

50ml water

FOR THE FILLING

200g minced lamb

2 shallots, finely diced

1 garlic clove, crushed

¼ teaspoon ground cinnamon

small bunch of fresh mint, leaves only, finely chopped

3 tablespoons hummus (see p.174 for the recipe)

1 HOUR IN ADVANCE

Using the dough hook on your food processor, combine the flour, salt, cardamom and pistachios, adding the eggs and water a little at a time to form a dough. Remove and knead the dough for 8–10 minutes, until silky smooth. Wrap in clingfilm and allow to rest for 1 hour.

TO MAKE THE FILLING

Combine all the ingredients, except for the hummus, in a bowl. Put to one side until ready to use.

TO MAKE THE MANTI

Cut the dough into 4 pieces. Lightly dust with flour, then pass each piece of dough through a pasta machine several times on the thickest setting, until it's beautifully smooth. Reduce the setting and pass through again, repeating until the dough is very fine. This process can be done with a rolling pin, but it is much more difficult and doesn't produce as fine results.

Cut the dough pieces into about 80 squares, roughly 3cm wide, or 3cm diameter rounds. Place a small amount of filling in to the centre of each square and top with a little hummus. Wet the edges of the squares with water, then pull the corners up and pinch the edges together to form a sealed pyramid-shaped parcel.

Place the manti on a lightly floured baking tray and refrigerate until ready to cook.

200g thick yoghurt or suzme
(strained yoghurt, see
instructions on p.183)

1 garlic clove, crushed

4 tablespoons olive oil

1 teaspoon sweet paprika

Bring a pan of salted water to the boil and drop in the manti, a few at a time, taking care not to overload the pan. Cook for 3 minutes, remove, drain and keep warm.

TO SERVE

Combine the yoghurt and garlic, and season to taste. Serve the manti hot, topped with a generous spoonful of yoghurt. Mix the olive oil and paprika together and drizzle all over the yoghurt.

For 8 to share

Kadaifi Wrapped Goat's Cheese and Cardamom Figs with Thyme Flowers

200g soft and mild goat's cheese

2 tablespoons mascarpone
cheese

2 tablespoons maple syrup

¼ teaspoon ground cardamom

300g kadaifi pastry

5 tablespoons melted butter

18 fresh ripe figs

50g pack of fresh thyme, with
flowers

1 egg yolk, beaten for brushing

Preheat the oven to 200°C fan/gas mark 7.

Combine the goat's cheese, mascarpone, maple syrup and cardamom in a bowl.

Carefully unfold the kadaifi and spread it out lengthways. Divide into 18 long strands – you will have some waste – and give each a generous brushing with the melted butter. Using a sharp knife, make a small cross over the top of each fig and squeeze open slightly, like a flower. Top with some of the cheese and maple syrup mixture.

Arrange the figs on a large, foil-lined baking tray and, starting at the bottom, wrap a thick single strand of butter-brushed kadaifi around each fig, leaving just the cheese-filled top exposed. Brush the strands of kadaifi with the egg yolk.

Bake the figs in the oven for 7–8 minutes, until the kadaifi is golden and the cheese melted. Remove from the oven and sprinkle with the thyme flowers before serving.

For 8 to share

Mung Bean Salad with Spicy Roasted Tomato and Honey Dressing

This dish is served daily at the Çiya restaurants of Kadýköy, Istanbul. Sometimes they add chargrilled red peppers or aubergines, turning this salad into a substantial meal.

FOR THE DRESSING

5 ripe tomatoes, halved

150ml olive oil

1 small garlic clove, crushed

2cm fresh ginger, peeled and grated

juice of 1 lemon

1 tablespoon runny honey

FOR THE SALAD

400g mung beans, soaked overnight

8 spring onions, sliced

3 plum tomatoes, cubed

small bunch of fresh parsley, finely chopped

½ teaspoon red chilli flakes

TO MAKE THE DRESSING

Preheat the oven to 180°C fan/gas mark 6.

Arrange the tomatoes on a roasting tray, season and drizzle with 1 tablespoon of the olive oil. Roast in the oven for 30 minutes, then remove and allow to cool.

Place the cooled tomatoes in a food processor with the garlic, ginger, lemon juice, and honey. Blend while slowly drizzling in the remaining olive oil until you have a smooth consistency.

TO PREPARE THE SALAD

Drain the beans and place in a pan. Cover them with cold water, bring to the boil, then reduce to a simmer and cook for 20–30 minutes, until soft. Drain and cool.

Place the cooled beans, spring onions, plum tomatoes and parsley in a large bowl and toss gently. Sprinkle with the chilli flakes, then drizzle with some of the dressing. You will have about 450–500ml of dressing, so if you have some left over, store it in a jar and refrigerate.

For 6 to share

Grilled King Prawn, Fig and Goat's Cheese Salad with Lemon and Honey Dressing

FOR THE SALAD

16 raw king prawns, shells and heads removed, de-veined

1 teaspoon ground sumac

1 teaspoon za'atar

5 tablespoons melted butter

4 fresh ripe figs, sliced into 8 wedges each

200g goat's cheese, crumbled

FOR THE DRESSING

3 tablespoons balsamic vinegar

2 teaspoons runny honey

2 tablespoons olive oil

juice of 1 lemon

TO SERVE

1 tablespoon black sesame seeds

a few apple blossom flowers or any herb flowers or leaves

TO MAKE THE SALAD

Preheat the grill to medium/high.

Place the prawns in a bowl with the sumac, za'atar and most of the butter. Mix well. Place the prawns on an ovenproof tray under the grill and cook for about 5 minutes, turning halfway through to cook evenly. Remove to a serving platter and brush with the remaining butter. Scatter with the figs and goat's cheese, and season to taste.

TO MAKE THE DRESSING

Mix together all the ingredients and drizzle over the prawns. Finish off by sprinkling with the black sesame seeds. Garnish with a few apple blossom flowers. If you cannot get any, you can use any herb flowers.

For 8 to share

Honey and Ginger Roasted Apricots with Ricotta on Green Peppercorn and Za'atar Spiced Filo

6 ripe apricots, quartered

3cm fresh ginger, peeled and grated

3 tablespoons runny honey

4 large rectangular sheets of filo pastry

50g melted butter

1 teaspoon green peppercorns, crushed

2–3 tablespoons za'atar

400g fresh ricotta, crumbled

Preheat the oven to 180°C fan/gas mark 6.

In a bowl, toss together the apricots, ginger and honey. Arrange on a baking tray and cook in the oven for 8 minutes, until just soft and lightly golden. Keep warm with the cooking juices until ready to serve.

Arrange a sheet of filo on your work surface, brush with butter and sprinkle with green peppercorns and za'atar. Top with another sheet of filo and repeat. Do this until all 4 sheets are layered on top of each other with the peppercorns and za'atar sprinkled in between. Cut the layers horizontally into 5 equal strips then vertically, so that you end up with 25 squares, although you actually only need 24.

Arrange the squares on to a greased baking sheet, then weight it down with another baking tray on top and place in the oven for 8–10 minutes, until crispy and golden.

TO SERVE

Crumble the ricotta on to 12 small serving plates, then arrange 2 ginger roasted apricots on each plate and garnish with a couple of the spiced filo pieces. Finally, drizzle with the apricot cooking juices.

Serves 12 as small bites

Nine Spice Lamb with Honey, Red Onion and Fig Compote

FOR THE MARINADE

juice of 1 lime

3 tablespoons olive oil

1 teaspoon baharat
(see p.173 for the recipe)

8 lamb chops, about 2cm thick,
fat trimmed off

FOR THE COMPOTE

20g butter

4 red onions, thinly sliced

½ teaspoon sugar

1 teaspoon honey

6 large fresh ripe figs,
cut into thin wedges

50ml sherry vinegar

1 tablespoon olive oil

2 tablespoons soy sauce

1 teaspoon za'atar

2 HOURS IN ADVANCE

Combine the lime juice, olive oil and baharat in a bowl. Rub into the lamb, place in a covered dish and leave in the fridge to marinate for 2 hours.

TO MAKE THE COMPOTE

In a pan, melt the butter on a low heat. Add the onions, sprinkle with the sugar and drizzle in the honey. Stir well, cover and cook for 15 minutes on a very low heat, making sure the onions do not colour. Remove the lid and add the figs and half of the sherry vinegar. Continue cooking, uncovered, until the liquid has almost evaporated. Add the remaining sherry vinegar and continue cooking until the liquid has evaporated. Finally, stir in the olive oil and soy sauce – you should be left with a sticky jam consistency. Remove from the heat, mix in the za'atar and allow to cool.

In a hot griddle pan, cook the marinated lamb chops on a high heat, for 2–4 minutes on each side, until golden brown. The cooking time depends on how you like your lamb, so cook for longer if you prefer them well done.

Arrange a spiced lamb chop on top of a generous helping of the red onion and fig compote.

For 8 to share

Lemon Thyme Infused Burrata with Honey, Berries and Balsamic Vinegar

500g burrata (or mozzarella if burrata is not available)

6 lemon thyme sprigs, leaves only

4 tablespoons runny honey

3 tablespoons almonds, toasted

400g mixed fresh berries

6 fresh ripe figs, cut into thin wedges

3 tablespoons balsamic vinegar

1 tablespoon icing sugar

1 DAY IN ADVANCE

Place burrata in a bowl with the lemon thyme leaves and 1 tablespoon of honey. Cover and leave in the fridge overnight.

TO SERVE

Spoon the lemon thyme infused cheese on to a serving platter. Drizzle with the remaining honey, then sprinkle on the almonds, berries and figs. Finish by drizzling with just a little balsamic vinegar and dusting with icing sugar.

For 8 to share

Orange and Honey Glazed Aubergine Rolls with Apricot and Cottage Cheese

FOR THE FILLING

zest of 1 orange

100g dried apricots, finely chopped

100g cottage cheese

2 tablespoons thick yoghurt or suzme (strained yoghurt, see instructions on p. 183)

1 teaspoon ground cumin

1 teaspoon ground sumac

¼ teaspoon cinnamon

50g pack of fresh parsley, finely chopped

FOR THE ROLLS

juice of ½ orange

1 teaspoon runny honey

2 tablespoons olive oil

2 medium aubergines, sliced lengthways into ½cm thick pieces

TO MAKE THE FILLING

In a bowl, combine the orange zest, apricots, cottage cheese, yoghurt or suzme, cumin, sumac and cinnamon, and season to taste. Add the parsley and mix again.

TO PREPARE THE ROLLS

Combine the orange juice and honey in a bowl, and put to one side ready to use. Lightly oil a griddle pan and place on a medium/high heat. Arrange the aubergine slices on the griddle and brush with the orange and honey mix. Cook for 2–3 minutes, then turn them over, brush again and cook for a further 2–3 minutes, until they are a golden brown. You may need to do this in batches if your griddle pan isn't big enough.

Spoon some filling on to each of the aubergine slices and roll each slice up to enclose the filling. Arrange the rolls on a serving platter and brush with the remaining orange and honey before serving.

Makes 16–18, depending on size of aubergines

Cardamom and White Chocolate Mousse

Make these a day in advance so they can chill overnight. Be sure to use the freshest,
free-range eggs.

4 eggs, separated

100g caster sugar

400g white chocolate, broken into
    pieces

300ml double cream

½ teaspoon ground cardamom

1 teaspoon cocoa powder,
    for dusting

1 DAY IN ADVANCE

In a food processor, blend the egg yolks with all but a tablespoon of the
sugar until thick and creamy.

Half fill a saucepan with water, bring to the boil and turn down to a simmer.
Put the chocolate into a heatproof bowl and place it on top of the simmering
water (it shouldn't actually touch the water). Give the chocolate a stir from
time to time, until it has melted. Allow the melted chocolate to cool, then
combine with the egg and sugar mixture.

Whisk the egg whites, adding the remaining tablespoon of sugar, and beat
until shiny.

Whip the double cream and fold into the egg and chocolate mixture. Finally,
gently fold in the whisked egg whites and the cardamom. Do not stir, beat
or whisk any further, as the object is to get as much air as possible into the
mixture.

Pour the mixture into 8 small ramekins and refrigerate overnight.

Dust with the cocoa powder before serving.

Makes 8

Sticky Honey, Pomegranate and Ottoman-Spiced Chicken Wings

4 tablespoons pomegranate molasses (see p.175 for the recipe)

juice of 1 fresh pomegranate

1 tablespoon runny honey

2 garlic cloves, crushed

1kg chicken wings

FOR THE OTTOMAN SPICE

1 tablespoon ground oregano

1 tablespoon ground mint

½ teaspoon ground black pepper

¼ tablespoon ground cinnamon

1 tablespoon ground cumin

¼ tablespoon ground ginger

¼ tablespoon ground fennel

¼ tablespoon ground allspice

½ tablespoon ground sumac

TO SERVE

seeds of 1 pomegranate

4 HOURS IN ADVANCE

Combine the pomegranate molasses, pomegranate juice, honey and garlic in a bowl. Add the chicken wings and thoroughly coat with the pomegranate marinade. Cover and refrigerate for at least 4 hours or overnight.

Meanwhile, mix all the baharat spices together.

Preheat the oven to 180°C fan/gas mark 6.

Arrange the marinated chicken wings on a large baking tray and sprinkle liberally with the Ottoman spice blend, putting aside a little for later. Roast for 30–40 minutes, until golden. Sprinkle on the remaining spice and pomegranate seeds just before serving.

Serve with Caramelised Onion Salad with Sumac and Pomegranate Dressing (see p.88).

For 8 to share

Pistachio Yoghurt Cake with White Chocolate and Cardamom Frosting

FOR THE CAKE

200g pistachios, ground

½ teaspoon ground cardamom

150g unsalted butter, cubed

225g self-raising flour

185g caster sugar

3 eggs

125ml thick yoghurt or suzme (strained yoghurt, see instructions on p.183)

FOR THE FROSTING

100g white chocolate, chopped

200g cream cheese

½ teaspoon rose water

1 tablespoon icing sugar

¼ teaspoon ground cardamom

1–2 small edible roses, petals only

1 tablespoon icing sugar (for sprinkling)

Preheat the oven to 180°C fan/gas mark 6. Butter and line a 20cm cake tin with baking paper.

Using a food processor, blend the ground pistachios, cardamom, butter, flour and sugar until you have something resembling breadcrumbs. Tip into a mixing bowl and combine with the eggs and yoghurt or suzme. Pour the mixture into the prepared cake tin and bake in the oven for 1 hour. Cover the cake with foil half way through cooking. Allow to cool on a rack.

TO MAKE THE FROSTING

Melt the chocolate in a bowl over a saucepan of simmering water, and allow to cool. In a separate bowl combine the cream cheese with the rose water, then add the cooled chocolate. Sift in the icing sugar and sprinkle in the ground cardamom. Mix well until you have a smooth cream.

Serve cake accompanied by the chocolate and cardamom cream. Sprinkle with edible roses and dust with icing sugar. Serve.

For 8–10 to share

Exotic Perfume & Delicate Fragrances
CINNAMON AND FLOWERS

Many years ago I was walking around a spice market in Mauritius, and there, amongst the heavenly scents, I bought a small bag of cinnamon bark. I put it into an ornate wooden box and brought it home with me. It has never been used, but still sits in its box on my desk; every now and then, I open it up and its exotic perfume instantly transports me back to that spice market.

Ground **cinnamon**, the most common form in which this spice is found, is a major constituent in many spice blends, baharat in particular. It's used across the Eastern Mediterranean in both sweet and savoury dishes, marinades, pilafs, baklavas and cakes.

What could possibly be more inspiring and exciting than using **flowers** in cooking? The vibrancy of their colour, the distinctive perfumed flavour, the delicate pretty fragrance: everything to delight the senses, alluring and seductive. Fresh or dried, flowers can lift the ordinary into the extraordinary.

Not all flowers are edible of course, but of those that are, nasturtiums, roses and lavender are the most common in Eastern Mediterranean cuisine.* Not to forget those that you will find in the herb garden: the purple flowers of chives, the snowy white coriander flowers, the violet basil flowers and the flaming orange courgette flowers, to name but a few.

As a child I knew nothing of strawberry jam; instead I grew up on rose petal jam for breakfast and rose petal or hibiscus ice cream as an after-dinner treat. Arguably, the best roses in the world come from the Eastern Mediterranean, and they are absolutely delicious as part of a spice blend to go with cauliflower or made into a syrup to accompany figs and ricotta.

*Only use commercially grown culinary flowers, or those from your own garden – others may have been sprayed with pesticides.

Orange blossom water is exactly what you would expect it to be. Distilled from an infusion of the fragrant blossoms of the orange tree, it is floral, bittersweet and, unsurprisingly, citrusy orange in flavour. It can be added to yoghurts and aioli, drizzled on to fruit salads and used in marinades. Readily available, it is usually very concentrated, so you'll need to go steady with it.

Lavender flowers can be used fresh or dried, and are fragrant, sweet, citrusy, even slightly woody in flavour. Add a touch to white chocolate, or even to chicken or lamb dishes. Seal the flowers in a jar of sugar for a couple of weeks and use the resultant lavender sugar in cakes. The dried flowers are much more potent than the fresh, so use a little at a time – you can always add more later.

Cauliflower with Rose Petal Spice Blend and Cardamom Hollandaise

FOR THE SPICE BLEND

- 1 tablespoon dried rose petals
- ½ teaspoon ground allspice
- ½ teaspoon ground cinnamon
- ½ teaspoon za'atar
- ¼ teaspoon ground cardamom

FOR THE CAULIFLOWER

- 2 tablespoons extra virgin olive oil
- 1 large cauliflower, cut into florets

FOR THE HOLLANDAISE

- 3 egg yolks
- 1 tablespoon lemon juice
- 175g melted butter
- ¼ teaspoon ground cardamom
  dried rose petals

TO MAKE THE SPICE BLEND

Combine the dried rose petals and ground spices together.

TO COOK THE CAULIFLOWER

In a large pan, heat the olive oil on high and sauté the cauliflower florets for 6–8 minutes over a medium heat, until golden brown. Place in a serving dish and sprinkle with the spice blend.

FOR THE HOLLANDAISE

Half fill a blender with boiling water, allow to stand for 3 minutes, then throw the water away and shake dry. Place the egg yolks and lemon juice in the warmed blender and blend for 10 seconds. With the machine still running, slowly drizzle in the melted butter through the hole in the lid. Blend until the sauce becomes thick and smooth. Finally, stir in the cardamom. Pour the hollandaise over the cauliflower, sprinkle with rose petals, and serve.

For 6–8 to share

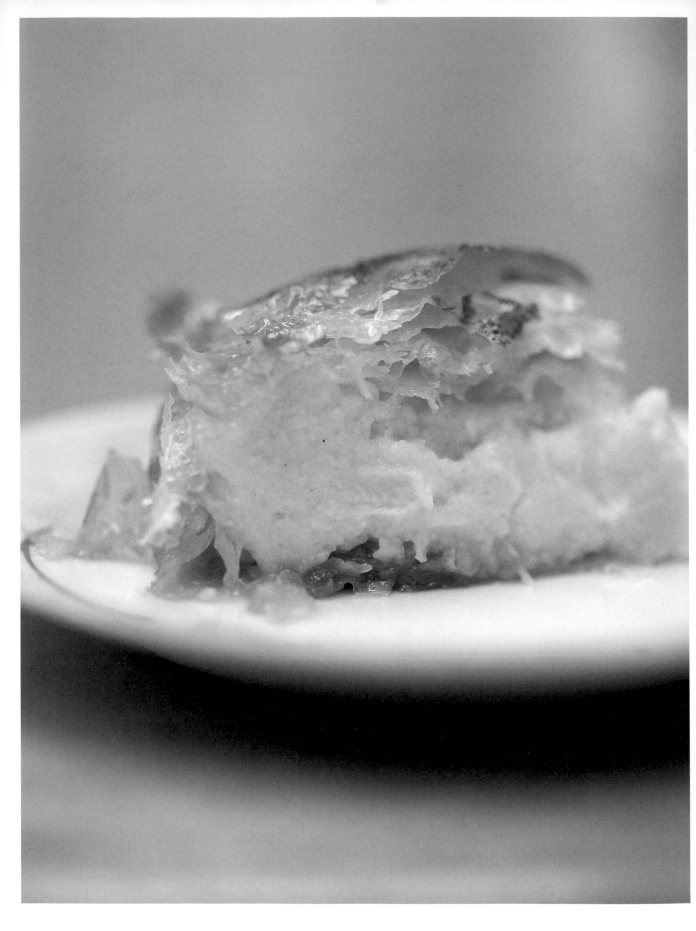

Lemon Vanilla Custard Baklava
with Orange Blossom Syrup

FOR THE SYRUP

250g caster sugar

250ml water

zest and juice of 1 small lemon

1 tablespoon orange blossom flower water

FOR THE BAKLAVA

4 eggs

200g caster sugar

750ml milk

200ml fine semolina

zest and juice of 3 lemons

2 vanilla pods, seeds scraped

100g melted butter, and extra for brushing

250g filo pastry

TO MAKE THE SYRUP

In a saucepan, dissolve the sugar in the water over a medium heat until it becomes syrupy. Add the lemon juice, zest and orange blossom water, stir and allow to cool completely.

TO PREPARE THE BAKLAVA

Preheat the oven to 180°C fan/gas mark 6.

Half-fill a pan (large enough to sit a mixing bowl on top of) with water and bring to the boil. Reduce to a simmer. Meanwhile, in a bowl, beat together the eggs and sugar. In a separate pan, boil the milk. Remove from the heat and whisk in the egg and sugar mixture. Stir in the semolina and transfer to a mixing bowl. Place the bowl on top of the pan of simmering water and stir for 10–15 minutes, gradually adding the melted butter, until the mixture thickens to a custard. Remove from the heat and stir in the lemon juice and zest and vanilla.

Butter an ovenproof dish, about 20 × 30cm. Lay in the first of the filo sheets, cutting or adding pastry to cover the base of the dish, then brush with butter. Repeat, brushing with butter as you go, until you have used half the sheets. Now pour in the custard, and layer in the rest of the sheets, again buttering between each sheet.

Using a sharp knife, cut any pattern you desire (diamonds, squares etc.) all the way through the pastry, then place in the oven for 15 minutes. Reduce the heat to 160°C fan/gas mark 4 and bake for a further 30 minutes, until golden. Remove the lemon custard baklava from the oven and pour the cooled lemon syrup over the top.

Allow to set for at least 4 hours and serve cold.

For 8–10 to share

Cinnamon and Black Sesame Crusted Cod with Baby Fennel and Radish Salad

FOR THE COD

800g cod fillet, cut into long thin strips, approx. 3cm thick

2 tablespoons olive oil

1 teaspoon ground cinnamon

4 tablespoons black sesame seeds

3 tablespoons olive oil, extra for cooking

FOR THE SALAD

8 baby fennel bulbs

16 pink radishes, thinly sliced

1 red onion, finely sliced

tomato and sumac dressing (see p. 179 for the recipe)

TO PREPARE THE COD

Season the cod strips with salt and pepper and brush with the olive oil. Mix the cinnamon and black sesame seeds together and use to coat the fish. Put to one side until ready to cook

TO MAKE THE SALAD

Slice the baby fennel bulbs wafer thin. Combine the fennel in a bowl with the radishes and onion.

TO COOK THE COD

In a frying pan, heat the olive oil and fry the cod strips for 2–3 minutes on a medium heat, turning until golden on all sides.

Serve the cod hot, on a bed of the salad and drizzled with Tomato and Sumac Dressing.

For 8 to share

Lavender Chocolate and Pistachio Mousse

250g good quality chocolate
      (70% cocoa solids), chopped

5 egg yolks

100g pistachios, finely ground

400ml whipping cream

¼ teaspoon lavender essence

50g pistachios, roughly chopped,
     toasted

TO SERVE

50g pistachios, crushed

4 HOURS IN ADVANCE

Using a double boiler or a heatproof bowl sitting over the top of a saucepan of boiling water, slowly melt the chocolate. Once melted, cool slightly and whisk in the egg yolks. Fold in the ground pistachios. At this stage your chocolate would look like it has curdled. Please don't worry, once you have added the cream, the chocolate will become smooth and silky again.

In a separate bowl, whip the cream to soft peaks. Add the lavender essence, then gently fold the lavender cream into the chocolate mixture.

Spoon into small glasses and top with toasted pistachios. Refrigerate for 30 minutes. If you chill overnight, then when serving, please allow to rest in room temperature for at least an hour.

TO SERVE

Serve cold, sprinkled with pistachios.

For 8 to share

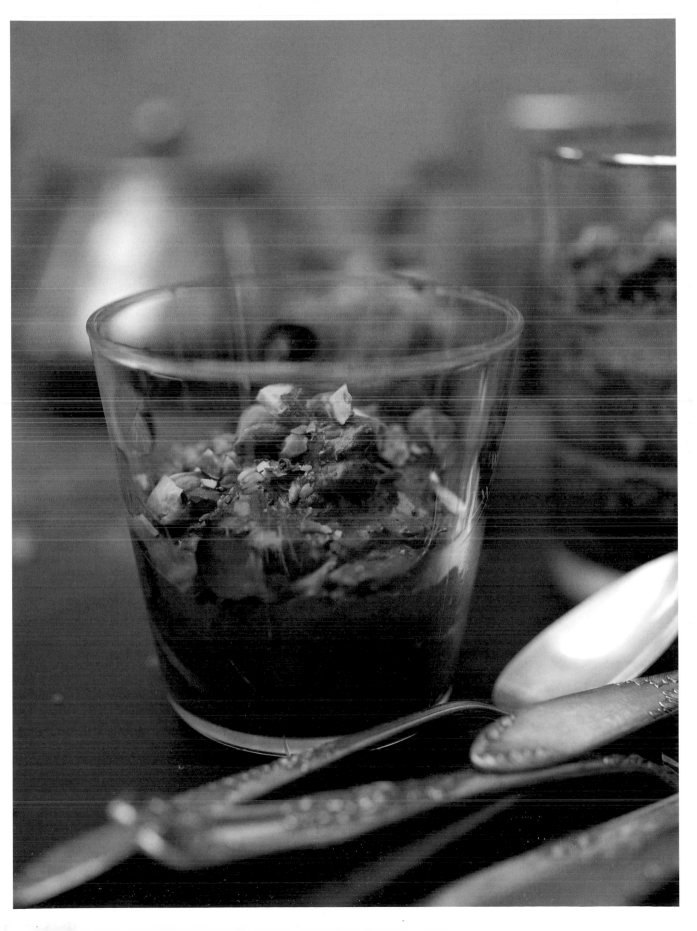

Roasted Figs with Orange Blossom, Passion Fruit and Mint Sauce

juice of 3 oranges

1 teaspoon orange blossom water

12 fresh ripe figs

3 tablespoons demerara sugar

TO SERVE

200ml thick yoghurt or suzme (strained yoghurt, see p. 183 for instructions)

6 passion fruits, pulp only

3–4 sprigs of fresh mint, leaves only, finely chopped

1 tablespoon icing sugar

Preheat the oven to 180°C fan/gas mark 6.

In a bowl, combine the orange juice with the orange blossom water. Cut a cross in the top of each fig and squeeze open the figs ever so slightly. You'll need a baking tray into which the whole figs will sit without much room to move about. Arrange them on the tray, then pour the orange juice mixture over the top of the figs and sprinkle with the sugar. Bake in the oven for 15 minutes. Remove from the oven and cool.

TO SERVE

Put the yoghurt or suzme into a bowl and combine with the passion fruit pulp and fresh mint. Plate up the figs and spoon some of the passion fruit yoghurt on top. Dust with icing sugar.

For 6 to share

Roast Potatoes with Rosemary, Shallot and Orange Blossom Aioli

1kg potatoes, peeled and cut into chunks

3 shallots

5 tablespoons olive oil

½ tablespoon sea salt

FOR THE AIOLI

4 sprigs of fresh rosemary, leaves only

150ml olive oil

2 egg yolks

juice of ½ orange

zest of 1 orange

½ teaspoon orange blossom water

Preheat the oven to 180°C fan/gas mark 6.

Cook the potatoes in a pan of boiling water until they are a little more than half cooked. Drain and tip into a roasting tin. Throw in the shallots, still in their skins, drizzle with the olive oil and season with the sea salt. Place in the oven for about 1½ hours, until the potatoes are golden and crispy. Remove the shallots after about 45 minutes. Once they have cooled enough to handle, squeeze the flesh out of the skins and put to one side.

TO MAKE THE AIOLI

Roughly bruise the rosemary leaves to bring out their flavour. Pour half the olive oil into a small pan and heat until just before it starts to really bubble. Remove from the heat and throw in the rosemary leaves. Allow to infuse for 1 hour, then add the remaining olive oil. Sieve to remove the leaves. Discard them and reserve the oil.

Place the egg yolks in a food processor with the shallot flesh. Purée until smooth and then, with the motor still running, slowly drizzle in the infused rosemary oil. Season, then add the orange juice, zest and orange blossom water.

Serve the roasted potatoes with the rosemary and roasted shallot aioli.

For 8 to share

Rose Water Infused Saffron and Cardamom Spiced Lamb Wraps with Tahini Sumac Mayonnaise

FOR THE LAMB

½ teaspoon black pepper, crushed

¼ teaspoon cayenne pepper

¼ teaspoon ground coriander

½ teaspoon ground cumin

¼ teaspoon ground ginger

¼ teaspoon ground cinnamon

⅛ teaspoon ground nutmeg

1.5kg lamb shoulder

6 threads of saffron

3 tablespoons rose water

3 tablespoons olive oil

8 cardamom pods, crushed

250ml water

FOR TAHINI SUMAC MAYONNAISE

3 egg yolks

150ml groundnut oil

150ml olive oil

1 tablespoon tahini

juice ½ lemon

½ teaspoon sumac

TO SERVE

24 small round flatbreads

I DAY IN ADVANCE

Combine the black pepper, cayenne pepper, coriander, cumin, ginger, cinnamon and nutmeg in a bowl. Rub the spices into the shoulder of lamb, then cover and place in the fridge overnight.

3 HOURS IN ADVANCE

Preheat the oven to 130°C fan/gas mark 2.

Soak the saffron threads in the rose water for 10 minutes. In a large ovenproof pan, heat the olive oil and brown the marinated lamb for 5–10 minutes, turning so that it is brown on all sides. Remove from the heat and add the saffron rose water, cardamom and water. Tightly cover the pan with foil, then place in the oven and cook for 3 hours. Take care when you remove the foil, as a lot of steam will have built up. The lamb, once cooked, should be falling off the bone.

TO MAKE THE MAYONNAISE

Whisk the egg yolks in a bowl, then, still whisking, drizzle in the oils a little at a time until you have a thick mayonnaise. Add the tahini and lemon juice and season to taste. Spoon into a bowl and sprinkle with sumac.

TO SERVE

Once the lamb has cooled, shred the meat. Warm the flatbreads then place a generous amount of meat in the centre of each one, spoon on some tahini mayonnaise and serve.

For 8 to share

Seven Spice Ground Beef and Courgettes with Garlic Yoghurt Sauce

FOR THE SEVEN SPICE

½ teaspoon ground cinnamon

¼ teaspoon ground allspice

¼ teaspoon crushed black pepper

¼ teaspoon ground cloves

¼ teaspoon ground coriander

¼ teaspoon ground nutmeg

pinch of white pepper

FOR THE BEEF

2 tablespoons olive oil

1 onion, finely chopped

600g ground beef

3 medium courgettes, cut lengthways into thin slices

small bunch of fresh mint, leaves only, chopped

FOR THE SAUCE

400g thick yoghurt or suzme (strained yoghurt, see instructions on p.183)

3 garlic cloves, crushed

8 fresh mint sprigs, finely chopped

4 tablespoons olive oil

TO SERVE

16 little gem lettuce leaves

Mix together the seven spices.

TO COOK THE BEEF

In a large, non-stick pan, heat the olive oil and sauté the onion for 2–3 minutes over a medium heat. Add the ground beef and brown for 5 minutes. Sprinkle in the seven-spice mix and cook for a further 8 minutes, stirring all the time. Next, add the courgettes, cover the pan and cook for a final 10 minutes. Season and stir in the fresh mint.

TO MAKE THE SAUCE

Simply combine all the ingredients in a bowl.

TO SERVE

Spoon the beef and courgettes on to the individual lettuce leaves, and top with the garlic and yoghurt sauce.

For 8 to share

Fig and Ricotta Tartlets with Rose Petal Syrup

150ml water

4 tablespoons caster sugar

1 tablespoon dried rose petals

8 fresh ripe figs, quartered

zest of 1 orange

100g shelled almonds

8 large sheets of filo pastry

4–6 tablespoons melted butter, for brushing

250g ricotta, drained

TO SERVE

handful of fresh rose petals

Preheat the oven to 180°C fan/gas mark 6.

In a small pan, combine the water with the caster sugar and dried rose petals, then gently bring to the boil. Reduce to a simmer and stir until the sugar has dissolved. Add the figs and orange zest and simmer for a further 5 minutes, until it turns to a thick syrup. Drain the fruit and reserve the syrup. Add the almonds to the fruit and allow to cool.

Lay a sheet of filo pastry on your work surface and brush all over with melted butter. Lay a second sheet on top, and again brush with butter. Repeat with 2 more sheets, then cut the 4 sheets into 8 equal squares. Repeat the process with the other 4 sheets of filo so that you have a total of 16 filo squares.

Spoon some ricotta on to each square and top with the fig and almond mixture. Make parcels out of the squares by lifting each corner of the pastry and pinching the edges. Leave a gap at the top.

Arrange the tartlets on a tray, brush with the remaining butter and bake in the oven for 12–15 minutes, until just golden. Remove and drizzle with the rose petal syrup. Scatter with some rose petals and serve.

Makes 16

Essential Accompaniments & Spice Blends

Black Sesame Crisp Flatbread

5g fresh yeast, or 3g dried yeast

4–5 tablespoons warm water

5 tablespoons olive oil

150g bread flour

flour, for dusting

3 tablespoons olive oil, extra for brushing

1 tablespoon black sesame seeds

TO SERVE

orange blossom honey

In a small bowl, stir the yeast into the warm water, then add the olive oil. Sift the flour into a separate bowl and pour in the yeasty water. Keep mixing until it turns to dough. Shape the dough into a ball and knead on a floured surface for 10 minutes, until it is nice and flexible. Shape into a ball and rest in a warm place in a covered bowl for 2 hours, until it has risen and doubled in size.

Preheat the oven to 200°C fan/gas mark 7.

Beat down the dough ball and knead again before splitting it into golf ball-sized pieces. With a rolling pin on a floured surface, roll each piece out until very thin. Brush with the extra olive oil, sprinkle with the sesame seeds and arrange on a baking sheet. Bake in the oven for 20 minutes, until just golden (see picture, p.123). If you prefer, you can cook on a pizza stone base.

Break into pieces and serve accompanied by the honey.

For 8 to share

Jerusalem Artichoke and Tahini Hummus

This hummus is made from Jerusalem artichokes instead of chickpeas, making the dish lighter.

500g Jerusalem artichokes, peeled and chopped

2 tablespoons tahini

2 garlic cloves, crushed

4 tablespoons lemon juice

3 teaspoons cumin seeds, toasted and ground

6 tablespoons olive oil

Place the Jerusalem artichokes in a pan and cover with cold water. Bring to the boil and cook on a medium heat for 12–15 minutes, until soft. Drain and cool.

Purée the artichokes in a food processor. Add the tahini, garlic, lemon juice and cumin. Switch your machine to pulse, then gradually drizzle in the oil and season.

For 8 to share

Aubergine and Tahini Dip

2 medium aubergines

2 garlic cloves, crushed

1 tablespoon olive oil

juice of ½ lemon

TO SERVE

1 tablespoon tahini

½ teaspoon sumac

½ red onion, finely chopped

Preheat the oven to 200°C fan/gas mark 7.

Place the whole aubergines on a baking tray and roast in the oven for 35–40 minutes, until cooked and soft. Once cool enough to handle, peel off the skin and blend in a food processor to a smooth purée. Add the garlic, olive oil and lemon and blend again.

To serve, spoon into a bowl, drizzle with the tahini and sprinkle with the sumac and chopped onion.

For 8 to share

Baharat Nine Spice Blend

This is a wonderfully warming and aromatic blend of spices that can be added to soups, tomato sauces, lentils and pilafs, and rubbed on fish, poultry and meat. Mix it with a little olive oil and it can be used as a marinade too. It can also be combined with sumac, saffron and turmeric. The proportions of the spices used in a baharat vary depending on whom you ask, but here's my special nine spice blend.

3 teaspoons mustard seeds

3 tablespoons coriander seeds

3 teaspoons fennel seeds

2 cinnamon sticks

3 teaspoons ground nutmeg

3 tablespoons cumin seeds

6 tablespoons dried thyme

6 tablespoons dried oregano

3 teaspoons black peppercorns

In a dry pan, toast the mustard, coriander, fennel and cumin seeds, along with the cinnamon sticks, on a high heat for 2–3 minutes then cool. Transfer to a bowl and add the rest of the ingredients. Crush in a pestle and mortar to consistency of coarse breadcrumbs. Mix well then store in a jar for up to 3 months.

Makes 30 tablespoons

Basic Skordalia

Skordalia is a Greek garlicky sauce or dip, usually made from either potatoes or bread.

2 slices of white bread, crusts removed

200g ground almonds

4 garlic cloves, crushed

200ml olive oil

juice of 1 lemon

Soak the bread in a bowl of water for 1 minute. Squeeze the bread dry and place in a food processor with the almonds and garlic. Process, drizzling in the olive oil, until you get a smooth and creamy consistency. Add the lemon juice and season to taste. If you prefer a thinner consistency, add about 50–100ml of vegetable or meat stock.

Makes approx. 300ml

Hummus

My hummus has always been deliciously light, silky and creamy (a nod to modesty here), laboriously made with chickpeas that have had their skins removed. An extremely tiresome job, but I believed it to be the best and only way to do it. Muhanad Jazier, chef at the Sednaya in Syria, showed me how wrong I was. So get out the bicarbonate of soda and a quantity of ice cubes, because you'll need them for this inspired method!

500g dried chickpeas, soaked
     overnight
¼ tablespoon bicarbonate of
     soda
4–5 ice cubes
4 tablespoons tahini
2 garlic cloves, crushed
     juice of 1 lemon

Drain the chickpeas and place them in a pan of fresh water. Add the bicarbonate of soda and bring to the boil, then continue to simmer on a low heat until the chickpeas are soft. You will need to skim the top of the water from time to time.

Drain the chickpeas and put a dessertspoonful of them to one side. Blend the rest of the chickpeas in a food processor, dropping in the ice cubes one by one. This method produces a wonderfully smooth texture and turns the hummus almost white.

Transfer the blended chickpeas into a bowl, add the tahini (here I've used 4 tablespoons, but if you prefer a less nutty flavour, use less), garlic and lemon juice, and season. Add a little more water if a thinner consistency is preferred.

Serve topped with the chickpeas put aside earlier.

For 10 to share

Pomegranate Molasses

This is a thick syrup made by boiling down pomegranate juice and sugar. It is sweet and sour at the same time. Delicious as a dressing, for marinating meat, or added to slow-cooked stews. Fairly readily available, but easy to make at home.

1 litre pomegranate juice (from a carton)

115g sugar

4 tablespoons lemon juice

In a large, uncovered saucepan, on a medium heat, stir all the ingredients until the sugar has completely dissolved. Reduce the heat to a simmer and cook for roughly an hour, or until the juice has a syrupy consistency and has reduced to about a quarter. Pour into a jar, allow to cool, then store in the refrigerator for up to 4 weeks.

Makes 250ml

Pesto

1 large bunch of fresh basil

2 garlic cloves

100g pine nuts

200g Parmesan cheese, grated

100ml olive oil

Place the basil, garlic, pine nuts and Parmesan in a food processor and season. Then, while blending, drizzle in the olive oil until you have a smooth paste.

Makes approx. 8 tablespoons

Tahini, Sumac and Lemon Sauce

4 tablespoons tahini

grated zest and juice of a small lemon

1 garlic clove, crushed

½ tablespoon ground sumac

3 tablespoons olive oil

120ml water

Place the tahini in a food processor, add the lemon zest and juice, along with the garlic and sumac. Process, adding the olive oil and water until you get a thin, single cream-like consistency. Season to taste.

Makes 250ml

Almond and Cumin Dukkah

Dukkah is an Egyptian spice and nut blend that has a fantastic crunchy texture.
Here I've mixed the dukkah with olive oil: a fantastic blend of flavours, perfect
in soups.

50g whole almonds, toasted

1 tablespoon coriander seeds,
toasted

½ tablespoon cumin seeds,
toasted

¼ tablespoon fennel seeds,
toasted

1 teaspoon black sesame seeds

Place all the ingredients in a food processor and blend until well combined.
I prefer a coarse consistency.

Makes 50g

Tahini and Cumin Dressing

3 tablespoons tahini

zest and juice of 1 small
lemon

1 garlic clove, crushed

1 teaspoon cumin seeds,
toasted and ground

3 tablespoons olive oil

100ml water

Blend together the tahini, lemon zest and juice, garlic and cumin in a
food processor. Slowly drizzle in the olive oil and water until you achieve
a consistency like single cream. Season to taste.

Makes 200ml

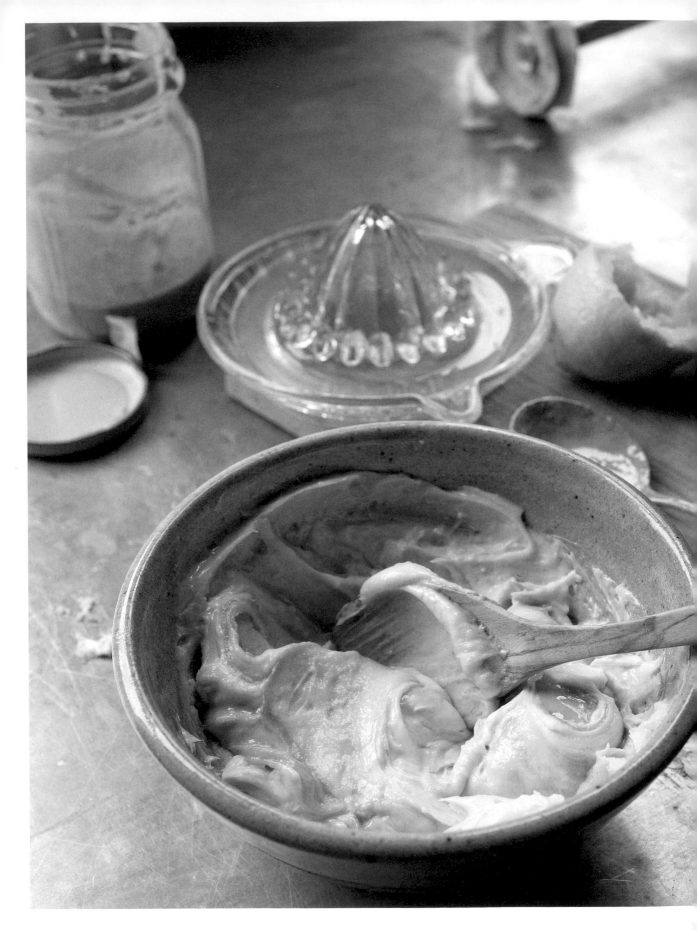

Tahini Mayonnaise

3 egg yolks
150ml groundnut oil
150ml olive oil
1 tablespoon tahini
juice of ½ lemon

Whisk the egg yolks in a bowl, then, still whisking, slowly drizzle in the groundnut oil and olive oil until you have a thick mayonnaise consistency. Add the tahini and lemon, and season to taste.

Makes 350ml

Tomato and Sumac Dressing

Simple and quick, this will brighten any fresh green salad.

1 large ripe tomato, skinned and very finely chopped
2 tablespoons olive oil
1 shallot, grated
1 teaspoon runny honey
1 garlic clove, crushed
3 tablespoons white wine vinegar
½ tablespoon ground sumac

Combine all the ingredients in a bowl and season to taste.

For 8 to share

Yoghurt, Mint and Garlic Sauce

200ml yoghurt
small bunch of fresh mint
1 garlic clove, crushed
2 tablespoons olive oil
handful of walnuts, finely chopped

Mix together the yoghurt, mint, garlic and olive oil. Transfer to a serving dish and sprinkle with the chopped walnuts.

For 8 to share

Za'atar @ Quince

Both a herb in its own right and a blend of dried herbs. Za'atar the herb has long green leaves and a thyme-like flavour. It is sometimes called wild thyme in English, and it grows along the slopes of the Syrian–Lebanese mountains. The za'atar referred to in this book, however, is the dried herb blend and I've included my signature recipe below. This is the main za'atar blend that I use at Quince restaurant.

4 teaspoons sesame seeds

4 tablespoons finely chopped fresh oregano

4 teaspoons dried marjoram

4 teaspoons ground sumac

1 teaspoon sea salt

4 teaspoons ground cumin

In a dry pan, lightly toast the sesame seeds on a high heat for 1–2 minutes. Then place all the ingredients in a blender and process until finely mixed. Store in a jar in the fridge for up to a week.

Makes 6–8 tablespoons

Lemon Thyme Za'atar

8 fresh oregano sprigs, roughly torn, with flowers if possible

8 fresh lemon thyme sprigs, roughly torn

2 tablespoons sesame seeds

2 teaspoons ground sumac

½ teaspoon salt

2 teaspoons ground cumin

Simply combine all the ingredients. Store in a jar in the fridge for up to a week.

Makes 6–8 tablespoons

The Eastern Mediterranean Store-cupboard

Aleppo chilli Mild, sweet, fruity and slightly smoky. You might have to look around for it, but it is available in many Turkish and Middle Eastern food stores, in red and green variations, usually as dried flakes. You can substitute mild red chilli flakes and a teaspoon of smoked paprika.

Almonds

Bulgur Finely ground, cracked wheat grains.

Cardamom Known as the 'queen of the spices', cardamom is used in both savoury and sweet cooking. You'll need both pods and ground.

Chickpeas Buy them tinned.

Cinnamon (dried)

Coconut milk

Coconut (desiccated)

Coriander (ground and seeds)

Cumin (ground and seeds)

Extra virgin olive oil

Fennel (ground and seeds)

Ginger (dried)

Honey (runny)

Kadaifi Kadaifi pastry is available in Middle Eastern and Turkish shops. It dries fast, so like filo pastry it must be kept under a damp cloth while you work with it.

Lavender (dried)

Marjoram (dried)

Mint (dried)

Mild chilli (flakes and powder)

Mustard (paste and seeds)

Nigella seeds These come from a flower that is a member of the buttercup family. They have a sharp, nutty, slightly peppery flavour. Make sure you toast them beforehand to release their flavours.

Nutmeg (ground)

Orange flower water Also known as orange blossom water. Orange flowers have a citrusy, bittersweet flavour and at the same time warm caramel notes. As well as pastries and sweet dishes, it is also used with chicken, pumpkin, and in pilafs. The secret is to use very little – too much and you will end up with a heavily perfumed dish.

Oregano (dried)

Orzo

Panko breadcrumbs These are readily available in most Asian shops, but if you can't get hold of them, toast ordinary breadcrumbs so they have a crunch to them.

Paprika The true aristocrat of spices, from the noble sweet varieties to the fiercely hot. It is hardly surprising, seeing that they use so much of it, that many people give the Hungarians the credit for introducing paprika to European cuisine, but it was in fact the Turks, via their trade routes, and from there to Hungary by way of the Balkans, who introduced the pepper to the Hungarians in the middle of the sixteenth century.

Parsley (dried)

Peppercorns (black and green)

Pine nuts

Pistachios Buy them whole, shelled and unsalted.

Ras-el-hanout A Moroccan spice blend usually made up of black pepper, coriander, ginger, paprika, allspice, cardamom, mace, nutmeg, turmeric, cayenne, cloves and rose petals. Available to buy in supermarkets and Middle Eastern stores.

Rose water

Saffron Can be bought in the form of threads, powder and liquid. Threads are the most expensive; a pinch of saffron is roughly 12 threads.

Sea salt

Sesame seeds Very high in oil content, with a nutty aroma. They're used to make za'atar, tahini and helva. You'll also need black sesame seeds for some of the recipes.

Sumac You'll see that this is a key ingredient for many of my recipes and fortunately it's more widely available now. Any good Middle Eastern food shop will sell it crushed or ground, and Waitrose stock it now. Sumac is the edible berry of a tree related to the mango. Sumac berries turn from dark pink to purple as they ripen, and as they dry and harden, they become the size of peppercorns. Sumac has a fruity aroma and citrusy flavour. Great with fish, salads and in pilafs.

Suzme (labne) Suzme is strained yoghurt, known in the Middle East as labne. When yoghurt is strained, and the mixture drains away, it becomes very thick. Left for twenty-four hours, it takes on the texture of cream cheese, thereby allowing it to be rolled in a variety of coatings, such as herbs, nuts and seeds. You should use a good-quality, full-fat plain yoghurt without additives. Prepare the suzme 1 or 2 days in advance of cooking with it. Place the yoghurt in the centre of some double-layered muslin or cheesecloth (approximately 30 × 30cm in size). Standing at a sink, twist the muslin around the yoghurt until you have a tight ball. Tie the top with some string and suspend the ball (I tie it to the tap) for a day or so. You will end up with yoghurt of a very thick consistency. It will be roughly half the weight you started with.

Tahini Sesame paste, used widely in Eastern Mediterranean and Middle Eastern cuisines.

Walnuts

Yufka Thin sheets of pre-cooked pastry, not dissimilar to filo, used in the cuisines of Turkey, Syria and Greece. Available in Middle Eastern or Polish shops, or online.

Index

apricots
  Honey and Ginger Roasted Apricots with Ricotta on Green Peppercorn and Za'atar Spiced Filo 139
  Orange and Honey Glazed Aubergine Rolls with Apricot and Cottage Cheese 144

aubergine
  Aleppo-Style Cumin Scented Baba Ghanoush 56
  Aubergine and Red Pepper Salad 49
  Aubergine and Tahini Dip 171
  Kadaifi-Wrapped Aubergine with Za'atar Rouille 15
  Orange and Honey Glazed Aubergine Rolls with Apricot and Cottage Cheese 144

avocado
  Crushed Broad Beans and Avocado with Parmesan and Sumac Biscuits 108
  Sumac Crab and Avocado with Tahini Dressing 122

Baby Carrot, Orange and Za'atar Hummus 5
Baharat Nine Spice Blend 173
baklava *see* pastries
beans
  Broad Bean, Wild Garlic and Fennel Dip 120
  Crushed Broad Beans and Avocado with Parmesan and Sumac Biscuits 108
  Fava Bean and Green Chilli Falafel with Yoghurt and Tahini Sauce 52
  Honey Mashed Broad Beans with Capers and Spring Onions 129
  Mung Bean Salad with Spicy Roasted Tomato and Honey Dressing 135

  White Bean, Parsley and Caramelised Fennel Salad with Lemon and Tahini Dressing 117
beef: Seven Spice Ground Beef and Courgettes with Garlic Yoghurt Sauce 166
begindi: Courgette and Dill Begindi 84
börek *see* pastries
Broad Bean, Wild Garlic and Fennel Dip 120
bulgur
  Sumac Tuna and Bulgur Tartare with Wild Rocket and Fennel Salad 82
  Swiss Chard Bulgur Pilaf with Caramelised Fennel and Za'atar 13

cake: Pistachio Yoghurt Cake with White Chocolate and Cardamom Frosting 148
calamari
  Cumin and Chilli-Crusted Calamari with Tahini and Chilli Mayonnaise 48
  Lemon Thyme Za'atar Fritto Misto 34
  Za'atar Crispy Fried Calamari with a Spicy Walnut Cream 24
Caramelised Onion Salad with Sumac and Pomegranate Dressing 88
Cardamom and White Chocolate Mousse 145
Cardamom Duck with Orange and Sumac Infused Sauce 113
carrot
  Baby Carrot, Orange and Za'atar Hummus 5
  Carrot, Cumin and Raisin Yoghurt Salad 41
  Chilled Carrot and Saffron Soup 33

Cauliflower with Rose Petal Spice Blend and
    Cardamom Hollandaise 152
cavolo nero: Skordalia Cavolo Nero Cakes topped with
    Shredded Duck Confit and Pomegranate 105
cheese
    Chilli-Scented King Prawn and Feta Guvech 65
    Duck, Haloumi and Green Chilli Spring Rolls with
        Sweet Potato and Almond Skordalia 39
    Gruyère and Mixed Herb Kadaifi Pies 98
    Haloumi, Walnut and Frisee Lettuce Salad with
        Nigella Seed Vinaigrette 86
    Kadaifi Wrapped Goat's Cheese and Cardamom Figs
        with Thyme Flowers 134
    Lemon Thyme Infused Burrata with Honey, Berries
        and Balsamic Vinegar 142
    Orange and Honey Glazed Aubergine Rolls with
        Apricot and Cottage Cheese 144
    Orange and Za'atar Marinated Haloumi with Tomato
        and Za'atar Dressing 29
    Summer Squash, Feta and Cumin Kofte with Wild
        Garlic Tzatziki 62
    Wild Greens and Feta Börek 94
chicken
    Chicken Stuffed Yoghurt and Cumin Pastry Börek
        53
    Chilli and Za'atar Chicken Wings 40
    Cumin-Scented Chicken Shawarma Caesar-style
        Salad 76
    Suzme and Chilli Marinated Chicken Shawarma with
        Aubergine and Red Pepper Salad 49
chickpeas
    Chickpea and Cumin Kofte with Tahini and Lemon
        Sauce 59
    Chickpea, Sweet Potato and Spinach Cakes with
        Creamed Parsnip and Coriander Dip 89
    Chilli Chickpea Street Pilaf 42
    Hummus 174
Chilled Carrot and Saffron Soup 33

Chilli and Za'atar Chicken Wings 40
Chilli Chickpea Street Pilaf 42
Chilli-Scented King Prawn and Feta Guvech 65
chocolate
    Cardamom and White Chocolate Mousse 145
    Lavender Chocolate and Pistachio Mousse 158
    Pistachio Yoghurt Cake with White Chocolate and
        Cardamom Frosting 148
Cinnamon and Black Sesame Crusted Cod with Baby
    Fennel and Radish Salad 157
cod: Cinnamon and Black Sesame Crusted Cod with
    Baby Fennel and Radish Salad 157
compote: Honey, Red Onion and Fig Compote 140
Coriander and Onion Whip 92
courgettes
    Courgette and Chilli Pesto 71
    Courgette and Cumin Falafel 47
    Courgette and Dill Begindi 84
    Crispy Herb-Coated Courgettes with Coriander and
        Lemon Confit Dressing 101
    Seven Spice Ground Beef and Courgettes with Garlic
        Yoghurt Sauce 166
crab
    Börek Rolls with Crab, Saffron and Fennel 6
    Cumin-Scented Jerusalem Artichoke Soup with Fresh
        Crab 72
    Fresh Crab and Coriander Gözleme 97
    Sumac Crab and Avocado with Tahini Dressing 122
Crispy Herb-Coated Courgettes with Coriander and
    Lemon Confit Dressing 101
Crushed Broad Beans and Avocado with Parmesan and
    Sumac Biscuits 108
Cumin and Chilli-Crusted Calamari with Tahini and
    Chilli Mayonnaise 48
Cumin Marinated Mackerel Fillets with Cumin and
    Lemon Thyme-Infused Shallot Purée 63
Cumin-Scented Chicken Shawarma Caesar-style Salad
    76

Cumin-Scented Jerusalem Artichoke Soup with Fresh Crab 72

Cumin-Spiced Rabbit with Hazelnut Skordalia Sauce 69

dips (see also hummus; mayonnaise; sauces)

Aleppo-Style Cumin Scented Baba Ghanoush 56

Aubergine and Tahini Dip 171

Broad Bean, Wild Garlic and Fennel Dip 120

Coriander and Onion Whip 92

Courgette and Dill Begindi 84

Creamed Parsnip and Coriander Dip 89

Crushed Broad Beans and Avocado with Parmesan and Sumac Biscuits 108

Cumin and Lemon Thyme-Infused Shallot Purée 63

Smoked Haddock and Sumac Whip 92

Wild Garlic Tzatziki 62

dressings

Coriander and Lemon Confit Dressing 101

Lemon and Honey Dressing 136

Lemon and Tahini Dressing 117

Nigella Seed Vinaigrette 86

Spicy Roasted Tomato and Honey Dressing 135

Sumac and Pomegranate Dressing 88

Tahini and Cumin Dressing 176

Tahini Dressing 122

Tomato and Sumac Dressing 179

Tomato and Za'atar Dressing 29

duck

Cardamom Duck with Orange and Sumac Infused Sauce 113

Duck and Black Sesame Za'atar Kleftiko 21

Duck, Haloumi and Green Chilli Spring Rolls with Sweet Potato and Almond Skordalia 39

Pistachio Dukkah-Crusted Duck with Sumac Onion Jam 93

Skordalia Cavolo Nero Cakes topped with Shredded Duck Confit and Pomegranate 105

Spiced Duck Rillette with Courgette and Chilli Pesto 71

dukkah

Almond and Cumin Dukkah 51, 176

Coriander Coconut Dukkah 114

Nigella Seed Dukkah 45

Pistachio Dukkah-Crusted Duck with Sumac Onion Jam 93

Seared Scallops with Hazelnut Dukkah on Sumac Onions 91

Sumac and Pistachio Dukkah Prawns with Tahini Sauce 107

Fava Bean and Green Chilli Falafel with Yoghurt and Tahini Sauce 52

fennel

Baby Fennel and Radish Salad 157

Börek Rolls with Crab, Saffron and Fennel 6

Broad Bean, Wild Garlic and Fennel Dip 120

Fennel and Preserved Lemon Salad 61

Swiss Chard Bulgur Pilaf with Caramelised Fennel and Za'atar 13

White Bean, Parsley and Caramelised Fennel Salad with Lemon and Tahini Dressing 117

Wild Rocket and Fennel Salad 82

Za'atar Red Mullet and Fennel Tzatziki Toasts 30

falafel

Courgette and Cumin Falafel 47

Fava Bean and Green Chilli Falafel with Yoghurt and Tahini Sauce 52

figs

Fig and Ricotta Tartlets with Rose Petal Syrup 167

Kadaifi Wrapped Goat's Cheese and Cardamom Figs with Thyme Flowers 134

Roasted Figs with Orange Blossom, Passion Fruit and Mint Sauce 160

Nine Spice Lamb with Honey, Red Onion and Fig Compote 140

flatbread: Black Sesame Crisp Flatbread 169

foie Gras: Spiced Quail and Foie Gras Filo Parcels 4

Fresh Crab and Coriander Gözleme 97

gnocchi: Potato Gnocchi with Coconut and Mascarpone
Sauce and Coriander Coconut Dukkah 114

gözleme *see* pastries

Grilled King Prawn, Fig and Goat's Cheese Salad with
Lemon and Honey Dressing 136

Gruyère and Mixed Herb Kadaifi Pies 98

guvech: Chilli-Scented King Prawn and Feta Guvech 65

haloumi *see* cheese

Honey and Ginger Roasted Apricots with Ricotta on
Green Peppercorn and Za'atar Spiced Filo 139

Honey Mashed Broad Beans with Capers and Spring
Onions 129

Hummus 174

Baby Carrot, Orange and Za'atar Hummus 5

Jerusalem Artichoke and Tahini Hummus 171

Jerusalem artichokes

Cumin-Scented Jerusalem Artichoke Soup with Fresh
Crab 72

Jerusalem Artichoke and Tahini hummus 171

kadaifi *see* pastries

kebabs

Sea Bass and Prawn Mini Kebabs with Tahini and
Chilli Sauce 58

Turkey and Pine Nut Kebabs with Saffron Mayonnaise
27

kleftiko: Duck and Black Sesame Za'atar Kleftiko 21

kofte

Chickpea and Cumin Kofte with Tahini and Lemon
Sauce 59

Summer Squash, Feta and Cumin Kofte with Wild
Garlic Tzatziki 62

lamb

Lamb Moussaka Rolls 55

Pistachio and Cardamom Lamb Manti 133

Rose Water Infused Saffron and Cardamom Spiced
Lamb Wraps with Tahini Sumac Mayonnaise 165

Nine Spice Lamb with Honey, Red Onion and Fig
Compote 140

Spiced Lamb Filo Cigars with Za'atar and Pistachio
Cream 26

Langoustine Salad with Preserved Lemon and Za'atar
Butter 17

Lavender Chocolate and Pistachio Mousse 158

Lemon Balm Sorbet, Black Sesame Macaroon Crumble
and Lemon Balm Oil 125

Lemon Thyme Infused Burrata with Honey, Berries and
Balsamic Vinegar 142

Lemon Thyme Za'atar 180

Lemon Thyme Za'atar Fritto Misto 34

Lemon Vanilla Custard Baklava with Orange Blossom
Syrup 155

Lentil and Parsley Tabbouleh with Wild Garlic and
Sesame Suzme 104

Lentil, Orzo and Pine Nut Pilaf with Saffron Onions 32

mackerel: Cumin Marinated Mackerel Fillets with
Cumin and Lemon Thyme-Infused Shallot Purée 63

manti: Pistachio and Cardamom Lamb Manti 133

mayonnaise

Rosemary, Shallot and Orange Blossom Aioli 163

Saffron Mayonnaise 27

Tahini and Chilli Mayonnaise 48

Tahini Mayonnaise 179

Tahini Sumac Mayonnaise 165

mousse

Cardamom and White Chocolate Mousse 145

Lavender Chocolate and Pistachio Mousse 158

Mung Bean Salad with Spicy Roasted Tomato and
Honey Dressing 135

mussels: Spicy Cumin Mussels with Pesto and Lemon-Infused Mascarpone 66

octopus
  Spaghetti with Octopus and Aleppo Chilli Sauce 75
  Sumac Octopus with Pomegranate 103
onions
  Caramelised Onion Salad with Sumac and Pomegranate Dressing 88
  Coriander and Onion Whip 92
  Fried Sumac Onions 119
  Lentil, Orzo and Pine Nut Pilaf with Saffron Onions 32
  Seared Scallops with Hazelnut Dukkah on Sumac Onions 91
  Sumac Onion Jam 93
Orange and Honey Glazed Aubergine Rolls with Apricot and Cottage Cheese 144
Orange and Za'atar Marinated Haloumi with Tomato and Za'atar Dressing 29

pastries
  Börek Rolls with Crab, Saffron and Fennel 6
  Chicken Stuffed Yoghurt and Cumin Pastry Börek 53
  Duck, Haloumi and Green Chilli Spring Rolls with Sweet Potato and Almond Skordalia 39
  Fig and Ricotta Tartlets with Rose Petal Syrup 167
  Fresh Crab and Coriander Gözleme 97
  Gruyère and Mixed Herb Kadaifi Pies 98
  Honey and Ginger Roasted Apricots with Ricotta on Green Peppercorn and Za'atar Spiced Filo 139
  Kadaifi Wrapped Goat's Cheese and Cardamom Figs with Thyme Flowers 134
  Kadaifi-Wrapped Aubergine with Za'atar Rouille 15
  Lemon Vanilla Custard Baklava with Orange Blossom Syrup 155
  Quick Cumin Börek 43

Spiced Lamb Filo Cigars with Za'atar and Pistachio Cream 26
  Wild Garlic and Cumin Choux Balls 44
  Wild Greens and Feta Börek 94
  Spiced Quail and Foie Gras Filo Parcels 4
  Za'atar Spiced Rabbit Gözleme 9
Pesto 175
  Courgette and Chilli Pesto 71
pilaf
  Chilli Chickpea Street Pilaf 42
  Lentil, Orzo and Pine Nut Pilaf with Saffron Onions 32
  Swiss Chard Bulgur Pilaf with Caramelised Fennel and Za'atar 13
Pistachio and Cardamom Lamb Manti 133
Pistachio Dukkah-Crusted Duck with Sumac Onion Jam 93
Pistachio Yoghurt Cake with White Chocolate and Cardamom Frosting 148
Pomegranate Molasses 175
pork: Spiced Pork and Cumin Sausages with Fennel and Preserved Lemon Salad 61
potatoes
  Potato Gnocchi with Coconut and Mascarpone Sauce and Coriander Coconut Dukkah 114
  Roast Potatoes with Rosemary, Shallot and Orange Blossom Aioli 163
prawns
  Chilli-Scented King Prawn and Feta Guvech 65
  Grilled King Prawn, Fig and Goat's Cheese Salad with Lemon and Honey Dressing 136
  Lemon Thyme Za'atar Fritto Misto 34
  Sautéed King Prawns with Orange and Sumac Butter 85
  Sea Bass and Prawn Mini Kebabs with Tahini and Chilli Sauce 58
  Sumac and Pistachio Dukkah Prawns with Tahini Sauce 107

Za'atar-Crumbed Prawn and Sweet Potato Cakes 22

pumpkin

Pumpkin Skordalia with Pine Nut and Nigella Seed
Dukkah 45

Roast Pumpkin and Almond Soup with Almond and
Cumin Dukkah 51

quail: Spiced Quail and Foie Gras Filo Parcels 4

Quick Cumin Börek 43

rabbit

Cumin-Spiced Rabbit with Hazelnut Skordalia Sauce
69

Za'atar Spiced Rabbit Gözleme 9

Raki and Honey Cured Salmon 130

red mullet: Za'atar Red Mullet and Fennel Tzatziki
Toasts 30

rice see pilaf

rillette: Spiced Duck Rillette with Courgette and Chilli
Pesto 71

Roast Potatoes with Rosemary, Shallot and Orange
Blossom Aioli 163

Roast Pumpkin and Almond Soup with Almond and
Cumin Dukkah 51

Roasted Figs with Orange Blossom, Passion Fruit and
Mint Sauce 160

Rose Water Infused Saffron and Cardamom Spiced
Lamb Wraps with Tahini Sumac Mayonnaise 165

Saffron Yoghurt Chicken with Cumin Salt Aioli 14

salmon: Raki and Honey Cured Salmon 130

salads

Aubergine and Red Pepper Salad 49

Baby Fennel and Radish Salad 157

Caramelised Onion Salad with Sumac and
Pomegranate Dressing 88

Carrot, Cumin and Raisin Yoghurt Salad 41

Cumin-Scented Chicken Shawarma Caesar-style
Salad 76

Fennel and Preserved Lemon Salad 61

Grilled King Prawn, Fig and Goat's Cheese Salad with
Lemon and Honey Dressing 136

Haloumi, Walnut and Frisee Lettuce Salad with
Nigella Seed Vinaigrette 86

Langoustine Salad with Preserved Lemon and Za'atar
Butter 17

Mung Bean Salad with Spicy Roasted Tomato and
Honey Dressing 135

Watermelon and Cherry Tomato Salad with Feta,
Almond and Za'atar Crumble 19

White Bean, Parsley and Caramelised Fennel Salad
with Lemon and Tahini Dressing 117

Wild Rocket and Fennel Salad 82

salsa: Pink Grapefruit Salsa 110

sauces (see also dips; mayonnaise)

Cardamom Hollandaise 152

Garlic Yoghurt Sauce 166

Hazelnut Skordalia Sauce 69

Olive Oil and Garlic Cream 96

Orange and Sumac Infused Sauce 113

Orange Blossom, Passion Fruit and Mint Sauce 160

Pumpkin Skordalia with Pine Nut and Nigella Seed
Dukkah 45

Spicy Walnut Cream 24

Sweet Potato and Almond Skordalia 39

Tahini and Chilli Sauce 58

Tahini and Lemon Sauce 59

Tahini Sauce 107

Tahini, Sumac and Lemon Sauce 175

Walnut and Roasted Garlic Sauce 121

Yoghurt and Tahini Sauce 52

Yoghurt, Mint and Garlic Sauce 179

Za'atar and Pistachio Cream 26

Za'atar Rouille 15

Sautéed King Prawns with Orange and Sumac Butter
85

scallops

Seared Scallops with Hazelnut Dukkah on Sumac
Onions 91

Sumac Scallops with Walnut and Roasted Garlic
Sauce 121

Sea Bass and Prawn Mini Kebabs with Tahini and Chilli
Sauce 58

Seared Scallops with Hazelnut Dukkah on Sumac
Onions 91

Seven Spice Ground Beef and Courgettes with Garlic
Yoghurt Sauce 166

Nine Spice Lamb with Honey, Red Onion and Fig
Compote 140

shawarma: Suzme and Chilli Marinated Chicken
Shawarma with Aubergine and Red Pepper Salad
49

skordalia 173

Hazelnut Skordalia Sauce 69

Pumpkin Skordalia 45

Skordalia Cavolo Nero Cakes topped with Shredded
Duck Confit and Pomegranate 105

Sweet Potato and Almond Skordalia 39

Smoked Haddock and Sumac Whip 92

sorbet: Lemon Balm Sorbet, Black Sesame Macaroon
Crumble and Lemon Balm Oil 125

soup

Chilled Carrot and Saffron Soup 33

Cumin-Scented Jerusalem Artichoke Soup with Fresh
Crab 72

Roast Pumpkin and Almond Soup with Almond and
Cumin Dukkah 51

Spaghetti with Octopus and Aleppo Chilli Sauce 75

Spiced Duck Rillette with Courgette and Chilli Pesto
71

Spiced Lamb Filo Cigars with Za'atar and Pistachio
Cream 26

Spiced Pork and Cumin Sausages with Fennel and
Preserved Lemon Salad 61

Spicy Cumin Mussels with Pesto and Lemon-Infused
Mascarpone 66

spinach: Chickpea, Sweet Potato and Spinach Cakes
with Creamed Parsnip and Coriander Dip 89

squid see calamari

Sticky Honey, Pomegranate and Ottoman-Spiced
Chicken Wings 147

Sumac and Pistachio Dukkah Prawns with Tahini Sauce
107

Sumac Crab and Avocado with Tahini Dressing 122

Sumac Octopus with Pomegranate 103

Sumac Scallops with Walnut and Roasted Garlic Sauce
121

Sumac Tuna and Bulgur Tartare with Wild Rocket and
Fennel Salad 82

Sumac-Crusted Tuna with Pink Grapefruit Salsa 110

Summer Squash, Feta and Cumin Kofte with Wild
Garlic Tzatziki 62

suzme

Suzme and Chilli Marinated Chicken Shawarma with
Aubergine and Red Pepper Salad 49

Wild Garlic and Sesame Suzme 104

sweet potato

Chickpea, Sweet Potato and Spinach Cakes with
Creamed Parsnip and Coriander Dip 89

Sweet Potato and Almond Skordalia 39

Za'atar-Crumbed Prawn and Sweet Potato Cakes
22

Swiss Chard Bulgur Pilaf with Caramelised Fennel and
Za'atar 13

tabbouleh: Lentil and Parsley Tabbouleh with Wild
Garlic and Sesame Suzme 104

Tahini and Cumin Dressing 176

Tahini Mayonnaise 179

Tahini, Sumac and Lemon Sauce 175

Tartlets: Fig and Ricotta Tartlets with Rose Petal Syrup
    167
Tomato and Sumac Dressing 179
tuna
    Sumac-Crusted Tuna with Pink Grapefruit Salsa 110
    Sumac Tuna and Bulgur Tartare with Wild Rocket and
        Fennel Salad 82
Turkey and Pine Nut Kebabs with Saffron Mayonnaise
    27
tzatziki: Wild Garlic Tzatziki 62

veal
    Anchovy and Parsley-Stuffed Veal Meatballs with
        Olive Oil and Garlic Cream 96
    Veal and Pistachio Mini Burgers with Fried Sumac
        Onions 119

Watermelon and Cherry Tomato Salad with Feta,
    Almond and Za'atar Crumble 19

White Bean, Parsley and Caramelised Fennel Salad with
    Lemon and Tahini Dressing 117
Wild Garlic and Cumin Choux Balls 44
Wild Greens and Feta Börek 94

Yoghurt, Mint and Garlic Sauce 179

za'atar
    Lemon Thyme Za'atar 180
    Za'atar @ Quince 180
    Za'atar Crispy Fried Calamari with a Spicy Walnut
        Cream 24
    Za'atar Red Mullet and Fennel Tzatziki Toasts 30
    Spiced Quail and Foie Gras Filo Parcels 4
    Za'atar Spiced Rabbit Gözleme 9
    Za'atar-Crumbed Prawn and Sweet Potato Cakes 22
    Za'atar @ Quince 180

Acknowledgements

What can I say about Jonathan Lovekin: a fantastic photographer and great friend, an integral part of making my cookbooks what they are.

It is one thing having a great idea, and quite another to put it into action: Caroline Gascoigne was the woman for the job. Thank you for your belief and attention to detail, without which this book would not have been as beautiful as it is.

I had always wanted to work with Susie Theodorou, one of the best stylists in the business, and I wasn't disappointed: great job.

Richard Marston I thank too: the design of Orient Express is pure class and elegance!

Natali of James Knight fishmongers: delicious fish and seafood, and she has always been there for me!

Last, but not least, thanks to Emma Rose, for coming back to help with the editing of this book. You know my work so well now!